ORIENTAL RUGS

ORIENTAL RUGS
A BUYER'S GUIDE

Lee Allane

With 80 illustrations, 40 in color

Thames and Hudson

Acknowledgments

I am especially grateful to Dominic Everest for his assistance in preparing this manuscript and for suggesting corrections and additions to the text.

I would like to express my gratitude to Hans Christensen for his considerable help during the writing of this book. Thanks are also due to Richard Lee, Arto Keshishian and the late L. Kelaty, and to other members of the trade too numerous to mention. A very special debt of gratitude must also be extended to Sam Wenneck for his help and advice on old and masterworkshop rugs.

I must also acknowledge the courtesy and co-operation of Rippon Boswell and Co. Ltd., for supplying the majority of the rugs used in this book. Other items were obtained from Dominic Everest Carpets Ltd., Carpet Export Import Ltd., and from the private collections of Jean-Pierre Mori and Glynis Bell. My thanks are extended to everyone concerned.

The sources of the colour plates are as follows: Einrichtungshaus Böhmler, Munich 11, 34; OCM (London) Ltd. 3, 7–9, 12, 14, 22, 31, 32; Neil Waving 1, 2, 4–6, 13, 15–20, 23–30, 33, 35–37; Rippon Boswell and Co. Ltd. 10, 21, 38–40.

Line drawings by Georgina Burrows

First published in the United States in 1988 by Thames and Hudson Inc., 500 Fifth Avenue, New York, New York 10110

Reprinted 1990

Library of Congress Catalog Card Number 88–50227

Printed and bound in Hong Kong

Contents

How to use this book

The range of oriental rugs on offer in a dealer's showroom or department store is overwhelming, and you may feel yourself to be at the mercy of the salesman. *Oriental Rugs: A Buyer's Guide* has been systematically organized to answer all your immediate questions, as well as to provide the one source of long-term reference you will ever need.

IF YOU ARE A COMPLETE BEGINNER, turn to Chapter I, which tells you what oriental rugs are and gives you a clear explanation of *essential rug-making terms*, as well as outlining the various *categories of rug*. Then read Chapter II, which concentrates on how rugs are made and describes how *techniques, materials and tools* affect the character and quality of particular rugs.

By now you will have a good picture of the basic background, and armed with this knowledge you should feel confident enough to contemplate **BUYING A RUG**. Chapter III will help you to choose a rug suited to your individual needs – you may want to make a worthwhile investment, or simply brighten up your home. It explains how to recognize particular types of rug,

and how to assess *quality and value for money*. You will find a guide to the *relative prices* of different rug groups, hints on *when and where to buy*, and advice on how to care for your oriental rug.

If you want to know more about a rug you already own, or simply want to develop a general interest in the subject, study the *design schemes* (described in Chapter IV), and the characteristics of rugs from the various producing countries (Chapter V). Chapters VI (on the *major weaving groups*) and VII (on *minor weaving groups*) give details on quality, design repertoire, colour schemes, price and retail value, which will expand your knowledge further.

Clear cross-references, supplemented by a thorough index, allow you to follow up a line of enquiry and to move easily from the text to the *line drawings*, *maps* and *colour plates* – each chosen to represent a particular design or type of rug typical of those currently available – offering instant visual access to the information you need.

The book will remain a valuable source of **PERMANENT REFERENCE**, whether in the store, in a museum, at auction or at home.

CHAPTER I

What is an oriental rug?

The term 'oriental rug' can be a source of some confusion to those unfamiliar with the subject. It literally means a rug manufactured in the Orient, and could legitimately be applied to any rug of oriental origin, regardless of its appearance or how it was made. In practice, however, the term is normally used only to describe hand-made rugs produced by traditional methods in the ancient weaving regions of Persia (Iran), Anatolia (Turkey), Afghanistan, the Caucasus, Baluchistan, Turkestan, China, India, Pakistan, the Balkans and parts of North Africa.

This vast geographical area – stretching from China to the Balkans and from India to the northern tip of the Caspian Sea – is inhabited by peoples of infinitely diverse cultural, religious and ethnic origins, whose only common feature (apart from occupying territories along the old silk route to the East) seems to be their desire and ability to elevate rug-making from a functional craft to an expressive and deeply satisfying form of art.

It can be difficult for Westerners to appreciate the importance of weaving in the East. Among many nomadic and tribal peoples it was often the only medium of creative release, and even in the more sophisticated cultures of Persia, China and Ottoman Turkey, weaving has always ranked alongside painting, architecture, sculpture and ceramics as a valid and celebrated visual art. A masterweaver in Persia or Anatolia was held in the same esteem as we hold Rembrandt or Vermeer, and even today there are some textile artists whose reputation and status are equivalent to those of any contemporary artist in the West.

Much of this veneration is due to the fact that rugs, in addition to their aesthetic value, have long been an integral part of the religious experience of the Islamic world.

Every good Muslim has his own special prayer rug, and Islamic religious symbolism is at the root of many of the most universal rug designs. It is for this reason that many experts prefer the expression 'Islamic textile art' when describing oriental rugs, despite the fact that many of the items covered by this description will certainly have been woven by non-Muslims and possess no trace of Islamic symbolism in their compositions. Nor does this expression take into account the elements of Buddhist, Taoist, Hindu and even Christian imagery found at the heart of many rug designs.

It is quite probable that religious symbolism was once exclusive to each particular faith. But centuries of migration, conquest, occupation, intermarriage, trade and cultural exchange – not to mention the tendency of artists to copy or reinterpret the most successful facets of other artists' work – have eroded much of this exclusivity. Today it is quite normal, and acceptable, for non-Muslims to weave prayer rugs purely for their aesthetic merits, and for faithful Muslims to use Hindu or Buddhist motifs to enrich their schemes. This interchange of visual ideas permeates every facet of the weaver's art, and is one of the prime reasons why all oriental rugs, regardless of their compositional differences, possess an underlying character that sets them apart from hand-made rugs produced in other areas of the world.

By virtue of being hand-made, all oriental rugs can be said to be unique – a weaver, no matter how hard he or she tries to follow a particular design, will invariably make small mistakes or innovations which will impart some individual flavour to the work – but it is rare to encounter a rug in which the weaver has consciously striven to express his own creative ideas at the expense of a traditional design. New designs have of course evolved over the centuries, and will no doubt continue to do so, but the Western passion for artistic freedom, novelty and personal expression is not shared by the textile artists of the East. It is perhaps because they are both unique and at the same time a faithful continuation of ancestral traditions that oriental rugs are objects of allure and fascination for the West.

In addition to their underlying similarities of character and appearance, oriental rugs are also defined by the manner in which they are made. They may be either 'hand-woven' (p. 24) or 'hand-knotted' (p. 25). The former are generally referred to as *kelims* or flatweaves, and are normally the cheaper and less frequently encountered of the two types. Hand-knotted rugs are known as pile rugs, or simply as rugs, and are generally regarded as the most important and aes-

thetically satisfying manifestations of the oriental rug-maker's art. They are usually very well made, and although there are always some relatively shoddy examples on the market, the vast majority are extremely durable; provided they are treated with a reasonable degree of care, they will last for many years. Evidence of this can be seen in the surprising number of items surviving from the late 19th and early 20th centuries, which one could be forgiven for thinking were only a few decades old.

In summary, we can say that an oriental rug, in order to be truly authentic within the generally accepted meaning of the term, must be either hand-knotted or hand-woven, originate from one of the traditional weaving regions and also follow certain ancestral patterns of composition and design.

Rug names and terms

A number of basic names, terms and expressions may be unfamiliar to people who are relatively new to the subject. Most will be explained in the chapters dealing with each particular aspect of weaving and design, but certain essentials need to be fully understood at the outset.

Spelling and pronunciation
The written languages used in most parts of the oriental rug-making world employ scripts that bear no resemblance to those of any major European language. Consequently, all translations of carpet names and terms are strictly phonetic, and it is therefore not surprising to find wide variations in the spellings of individual towns, weaving groups and designs. The most common variations are those which involve similar vowel sounds: the letters 'a' and 'e', for example, are frequently interchanged (e.g. Meshed or Mashad), as are 'i' and 'e' (Milas or Melas). Similarly, the letters 'y' and 'i' may be used to represent the same sound (Kaiseria or Kayseria). Consonants are not normally interchangeable and are therefore more consistently applied, although there are two main exceptions. The first concerns the interchange of 'k' and 'q' (Qashga'i or Kashga'i, or even Kashgay). The second

involves the juxtaposition of two consonants not usually placed together in an attempt to reproduce a sound peculiar to the original language (e.g., the 'kh' sound in Bakhtiari or Bakhshaish); the two consonants used in this way may vary, or one of them may be left out altogether.

Pronunciation is relatively straightforward: there are no silent letters and each syllable is pronounced with equal stress. For example, Daghestan is pronounced 'Dag-hess-tan', and Nain, 'Nah-een'.

How rugs get their names
Place of origin or tribe Most oriental rugs derive their names either from their place of origin or, in the case of nomadic items, the weaving tribe. A rug made in the Persian town of Kashan is therefore known as a Kashan, and an item woven by the Belouch nomads is called a Belouch. With nomadic items, it is not uncommon for a rug to be known by both the name of the specific weaving tribe (or sub-tribe) and the overall tribal grouping. Consequently, the vast majority of rugs made in Central Asia are collectively referred to as Turkomans, regardless of the fact that they are made by a number of specific tribes (Beshir, Tekke, Ersari, etc.), while individual items may be

marketed under either the collective Turkoman heading or the name of the actual weaving tribe. Usually, the collective heading is only employed when the exact attribution of a particular item is uncertain. The same is true of town and village rugs, and individual items that clearly originate from a broadly defined area or region, but can not be tied down to a specific village or town will be marketed under the name of the general location. Consequently, an item originating from somewhere within the Persian province of Khorassan will simply be called a Khorassan. It is also quite normal for the rugs of small villages to be marketed under the name of the nearest large rug-producing town, providing of course that there are strong similarities between their rugs; items produced in villages around the Persian city of Hamadan, for example, may be collectively referred to as Hamadans.

Design Some of the more famous names in oriental rugs, in particular Herati and Mir, refer to the design, rather than the place where they were made. These designs may be more closely associated with some weaving groups than others (e.g., Ferahan and Mal-e-mir), and it is not unusual for the names of the design and the weaving group to be interchanged. There is also a growing tendency in the carpet trade to market rugs from certain parts of the world under the name of the weaving group whose design has been used, rather than that of the group who actually made the rug. This is particularly true of items from India and Pakistan, which are often sold under the names of famous Persian or Turkoman weaving groups, and it is sometimes a matter of confusion whether the name Isfahan, for example, refers to a rug made in the Persian town of Isfahan or whether it is an Indian or Pakistani rug composed in a traditional Isfahan scheme. It is extremely important, because of the price and resale differences between items from the various countries, to ask specifically whether the name used refers to the rug's place of origin or its design.

Prefixes These generally denote that an item bearing the name of one weaving group was in fact made by another. For example, a rug made in the Kars region of Anatolia (Turkey) in a traditional Kazak (Caucasian) design will normally be referred to as a Kars Kazak. Usually, the first name or prefix indicates the weaving group and the second refers to the group whose design has been employed. The prefixes most commonly used in this way are Kars, Indo and Mori.

Kars Region in eastern Anatolia, close to the Caucasian border. Its use as a prefix is normally confined to Anatolian items made in Caucasian designs.

Indo As the name suggests, this simply means made in India and is used in conjunction with the names of mainly Persian weaving groups (Indo Isfahan, Indo Heriz, etc.).

Mori Indicates that rugs based on the traditional designs of weaving groups in other countries (in particular the Persian town of Kashan and the Turkoman Bokharas) were made in Pakistan.

In addition, prefixes are used to indicate that a particular rug was woven by a subgroup of a better known major group. For example, an Haft Bolah Belouch is a Belouch rug made by the Haft Bolah sub-tribe; a Ravar Kerman is a Kerman rug made in the nearby village of Ravar.

Prefixes are not always used, and a direct inquiry should be made if there is any doubt as to where or by whom a particular rug was made.

Rugs and carpets

The terms 'rug' and 'carpet' are normally used to denote size – a carpet being any rug with a surface area in excess of 4.4 m², and whose length is not more than $1\frac{1}{2}$ times its width, i.e., $9' \times 6'$ (2.74×1.83 m) or $12' \times 8'$ (3.66×2.44 m). This distinction is not always made, however. In the United States, and many other countries, 'rug' is used to describe any item, regardless of size, whereas anything sold in Britain or the British Commonwealth is usually clearly identified either as a carpet or a rug.

Some specific types of rug and rug designs have also been traditionally referred to either as carpets or rugs, totally independent of size. Prayer rugs, for example, are never referred to as carpets, and anything employing a hunting design would tend to be called a hunting carpet rather than a hunting rug. Similarly, experts will talk about Persian carpets and Anatolian (Turkish) rugs, regardless of the fact that both countries produce items in all sizes, shapes and designs; this is probably because Persia is most famous for its magnificent Court carpets, while Anatolia is viewed as the home of the prayer rug. In practice, the two terms are employed very loosely, and are often interchangeable, but to avoid confusion the term 'rug' will be used as a description throughout this book, and 'carpet' will be reserved for items of the appropriate size or type.

Runners, strips and mats

The first two terms describe rugs which are long and narrow – usually where the length is over $2\frac{1}{2}$ times the width – and are often used in place of the word 'rug' (i.e., a Shirvan runner or Yahyali strip). There are no rules defining the distinction between runners and strips, but it is generally accepted that a runner is relatively large (hallway or corridor size), whereas a strip is rarely more than $3' \times 1'$ (0.9 × 0.3 m). The term 'mat' can be applied to any small rug, but usually refers only to those whose dimensions are less than $c.\ 2' \times 2'$ (0.6 × 0.6 m).

Classifying oriental rugs

Oriental rugs can be classified according to a number of criteria – design, colours, materials, price, etc. – but arguably the most useful, and certainly the most widely employed, methods of classification are by country of origin, weaving group and general weaving category.

Country of origin

Classifying rugs according to their country of origin is both logical and necessary, particularly as discrepancies in exchange rates, import tariffs and production costs can make a considerable difference to the prices asked in shops for very similar items from different countries; but this method has its limitations. National boundaries have changed, sometimes dramatically, over the last hundred years, and some traditional rug-producing countries have since been absorbed into modern states. In addition, some of the countries whose boundaries have remained relatively stable produce such a wide variety of items, stemming from the diverse cultural, religious and ethnic backgrounds of their people, that it is impossible to categorize their rugs under one homogeneous style.

In order to limit the degree of confusion that these factors may cause, the names of the traditional weaving areas (Persia, Anatolia, the Caucasus, Afghanistan, Turkestan, etc.) have been used when discussing the weaving, history or design influences of their rugs, and the names of the modern states have been used when referring to

purely commercial factors, such as import tariffs, government actions and subsidies.

Traditional name	Modern name
Persia	Iran
Anatolia	Turkey
Caucasus	Soviet Union
West Turkestan and the western territories of the Turkoman nomads	Mainly in the Soviet Union, but also in some parts of Afghanistan and north-east Iran
East Turkestan and the eastern territories of the Turkoman nomads	China
Tibet and Mongolia	China
Baluchistan and territories of the Belouch nomads	Afghanistan, north-east and eastern Iran

Weaving group

The term 'weaving group' can be applied to any town, village or tribe within the oriental weaving region, which produces its own hand-made rugs, but it is normally only used in the context of the older, more traditional weaving centres in which rugs possess their own distinctive characteristics. Consequently, very few weaving centres in India or Pakistan can be said to constitute individual weaving groups. Similarly, one cannot talk about contemporary Chinese, Russian or Balkan weaving groups, because there is usually little or no difference in the character and appearance of rugs made in the various centres throughout each country.

In addition to classifying specific weaving centres or tribes, the term may also be used in a broader sense to encompass any collection of tribes or villages which combine the same ethnic origins, or general location, with an underlying uniformity in their rugs. It is not enough to have only one of these criteria in common. For example, an Indian village producing Kashan-style rugs cannot be said to be part of the Kashan weaving group; nor can the Persian towns of Kashan and Arak be placed together, despite their relative proximity, because of the strong dissimilarities in their rugs.

Weaving category

Oriental rugs can also be split into four broad categories which relate to their overall characteristics and appearance, rather than to where or by whom they were made. Each of these categories – nomadic, village, workshop and masterworkshop – has its own special qualities and appeal; people who like nomadic rugs, for example, will tend to appreciate them as a whole, regardless of whether they originate from Persia, Anatolia or Afghanistan. A basic knowledge of the specific characteristics of each category is a crucial first step in the understanding and appreciation of oriental rugs. The boundaries, however, are not always clearly defined, and while the vast majority of items fall clearly into one category, some could reasonably be placed on either side of the dividing line.

Nomadic rugs (pls. 1–12) Produced by nomadic and semi-nomadic tribesmen (semi-nomads spend part of the year in villages or settled camps) whose life has traditionally revolved around breeding sheep, weaving rugs and raiding their neighbours' camps. Their passion for raiding has declined in recent years, but in most other respects their lifestyles have changed little in centuries, and the rugs they make today remain faithful to their ancestors' methods of weaving and repertoire of designs. In nomadic cultures, rug-making is a female preserve, and prowess at weaving is a major factor in determining personal status, as

well as being an expression of the artistic, religious and cultural heritage of the tribe. Young girls are taught the skills from an early age, and it is customary in most tribes for them to display their first solo works as proof of their eligibility for marriage and elevation to the status of womanhood. Weaving also plays an essential part in the practical life of the tribe, providing the floor coverings, tent hangings, bags and functional artefacts that constitute the furniture and furnishings of the nomadic way of life.

The rigours of their existence place severe restrictions on the kind of rugs that can be made. It is rare for a tribe to spend more than a few months in any one place; consequently, any rug that is unfinished when the tribe moves has to be fastened tightly to the loom and transported in its entirety to the next encampment. The large looms needed to make carpet-size items are difficult to transport, and so the vast majority of their output consists of small- and medium-size rugs and a range of bags and other tribal artefacts.

Authentic nomadic weaving is now confined to Persia, Afghanistan and Anatolia (of the major rug-producing areas), although its influence can be found in the workshop items of other regions, particularly the Soviet Union. Although most nomadic tribes have a long history of weaving rugs specifically for trade, a number of items coming onto the Western market may well have been made originally for personal use.

Nomadic designs are woven from memory and are usually characterized by their overall compositional boldness, simplicity of colouring (sometimes employing only 3 or 4 hues to create a dramatic yet dignified effect) and the use of mainly geometric motifs and forms. Curved lines are rare, and even in the most intricate and subtle of patternings an essence of angularity usually underpins the scheme. Perhaps the most distinctive characteristic is the frequent presence of strong totemistic elements, ranging from a variety of traditional symbols for warding off the 'evil eye' to specific tribal motifs (usually of plant or animal derivation) which act as both identifying 'insignia', and 'talismen' to protect and increase the power of the tribe. Whether the

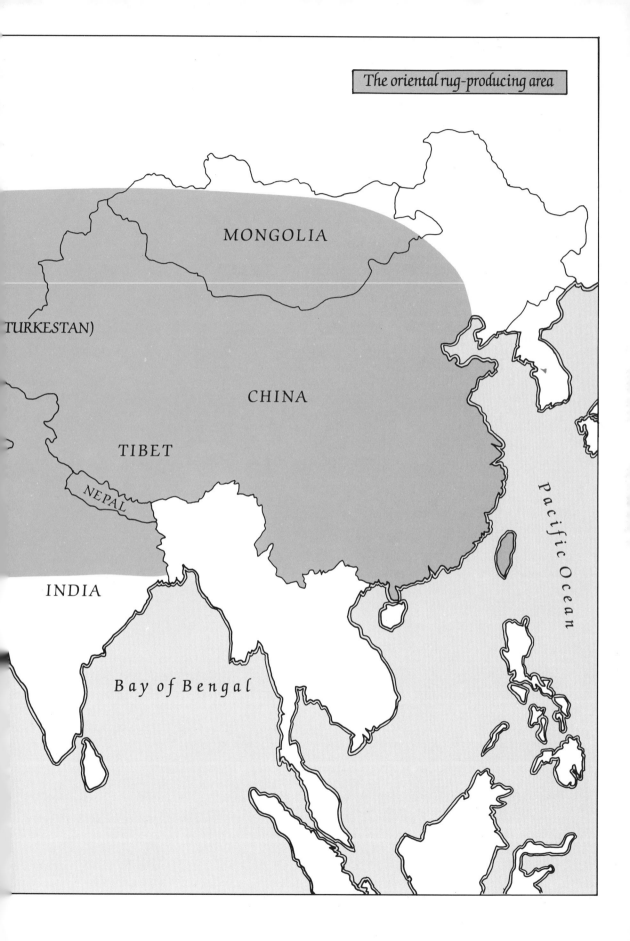

The oriental rug-producing area

(TURKESTAN)

MONGOLIA

CHINA

TIBET

NEPAL

INDIA

Bay of Bengal

Pacific Ocean

weavers of today are aware of the symbolic meaning of their designs – or whether they simply reproduce them out of a general reverence for tradition – is a matter of considerable debate, but there is no doubt that the symbolic potency of nomadic designs is one of the major reasons for their growing popularity in the West.

When assessing a nomadic rug do not be too concerned with technical perfection, variations in colouring (abrashes) or a lack of symmetry in the overall composition. Occasional discordances in the form of individual motifs are relatively commonplace and often help to give the rug its particular charm. Equally, do not expect to find the same fineness of knotting in a nomadic item as in a rug of workshop origin, although some nomadic rugs are surprisingly finely knotted and consistent in their designs. Most are woven on woollen warps and wefts (p. 20) – not the most stable of foundation materials – and consequently tend to lose their shape. This can largely be avoided by careful handling, and many connoisseurs believe that a slight structural asymmetry adds to the rug's overall character. The pile wool, however, is usually of extremely good quality.

In contrast, the qualities to look for are rather more difficult to define, and largely consist of a general character and appearance that springs from the individual interpretation of traditional tribal designs. Unlike her workshop counterparts, the nomadic weaver shares the same ancestral heritage as her designs, and is consequently a part of the traditions that pervade everything she weaves. This cultural empathy inevitably leads to a fusion of individual expression and tradition that is far more pronounced than that found in any other category of oriental rug.

Village rugs (pls. 8–24) The term is not used in its literal sense to describe items produced in villages as opposed to cities or towns, but is applied more specifically to a broad category of rugs sharing common features of construction, character and design. In the generally accepted hierarchy of oriental weaving, village rugs fall somewhere between nomadic and workshop products. This is hardly surprising, since most villages have long occupied the middle ground between nomadic traditions and the evolving sophistication of the towns, often acting as a buffer between the two alien ways of life. Many nomads have settled in villages, bringing with them their ancestral compositions and weaving techniques, and few villages have escaped the broader cultural and rug-making influences spreading outwards from the towns. The result is a wonderfully varied fusion of these two dichotomous styles.

Many villages, especially in Persia, which have long been associated with highly sophisticated work, have either ceased weaving altogether or produce so few examples that they now have only an historic relevance to the contemporary scene. There are still a number of village groups which produce items of exceptional intricacy, but the majority possess the rough-hewn beauty and coarser weave associated with nomadic rugs. They are usually sturdily – rather than finely – knotted in good quality wool which, because of the thickness of the yarns, precludes the possibility of intricate, curvilinear designs.

Contemporary village weaving is largely confined to Persia, Anatolia and, to a lesser extent, Afghanistan. The overwhelming majority of village-style items from the other rug-producing countries are in fact of workshop origin. However, items produced in some Persian cities and towns (e.g., Hamadan and Shiraz) possess all the structural and visual characteristics of village weaving, and are consequently referred to as village rugs.

Village designs are extremely varied, drawing inspiration from both nomadic and workshop schemes, with a greater diversity of compositions than in any other category. The most popular designs are prayer-rug, medallion and repeating geometric forms, with a variety of vegetal-inspired infill decorations; numerous interpretations of *boteh*, *herati*, tree-of-life and allover floral schemes are also extremely popular (*see* Chapter IV). Some weaving groups favour bold, relatively simple designs, while others produce works of considerable intricacy and sophistication. They usually share with the nomads a certain angularity in their overall compositions and articulation of forms. In some groups this use of geometric shapes is predetermined by the coarseness of the weave, but in others it reflects a conscious desire to adhere to traditional forms.

When assessing a village rug, first take into account the nature and complexity of the design. As a general rule, rugs employing bolder, more overtly geometric compositions should be judged by the same criteria as nomadic rugs, particularly if they are also dyed in a limited palette of austere or primary shades. In contrast, the finest and most prestigious village rugs should be judged by the same standards as workshop items.

Workshop rugs (pls. 22–37) Made in workshops of varying sizes and degrees of sophistication throughout the entire weaving area. They are distinguished from village and nomadic rugs in both their overall character and appearance, and in the way they are made. This normally involves working either from a design laid out on squared paper or under the direction of an overseer (or *salim* in Persian), who systematically calls out the colour of each knot as it is required. This process of manufacture inevitably leads to a certain loss of spontaneity in the design but, as compensation, makes it possible for far more technically exacting compositions to be achieved. Unlike village and nomadic weaving, which is normally the sole preserve of women and carries with it no personal prestige outside the village or tribe, workshops employ both men and women, and exceptionally talented weavers can earn more widespread acclaim and far greater financial rewards. These more skilful practitioners are sometimes recruited by rival workshops, or set up workshops of their own, and there is generally a more systematic and businesslike approach to making and selling rugs. This does not mean that the rugs are in any way less authentic than those produced by village or nomadic groups. Contemporary workshop rugs stem from a parallel tradition stretching back into antiquity, and many of the items produced during the last 30 years (particularly those from the major weaving centres of Persia and

A design drawn on squared paper.

Anatolia) rank among the finest ever made (p. 95).

Workshop designs are generally more finely knotted and elaborate than those found on village or nomadic rugs, and can be roughly divided into two overall types: those that are essentially geometric in character and those that employ more flowing, curvilinear forms. The geometric compositions are derived from traditional village and nomadic designs and are widely used in the Soviet Union, Pakistan and Afghanistan. Curvilinear designs are found in rugs produced throughout the entire oriental weaving area and usually employ naturalistic floral elements, which range from the essentially floral Shah Abbas, garden or vase compositions, to the incorporation of flower, leaf or stem motifs into the infill decorations or border arrangements of allover and medallion designs.

In Persia and Anatolia each workshop group (Isfahan, Kashan, Hereke, etc.) has evolved its own characteristic style and, with a little experience, people relatively new to the subject should be able to distinguish the most typical examples of one group from those of another. In contrast, rugs produced in India, Pakistan, the Soviet Union, Afghanistan and the Balkans are often extremely difficult to distinguish from one another because they are usually based on the same range of traditional Persian, Turkoman or Caucasian designs; often the only difference in their appearance is the fineness of the knotting and the skill with which the composition has been achieved. The same is true of Chinese rugs, which are made in both Persian and traditional Chinese designs.

When assessing a workshop rug judge each item on its individual merit – more so than with any other category – because of the extremes in quality found in this range. At the lower end of the scale the items may be far shoddier than even the cheapest village or nomadic rug; at the higher end, one can find work of the most outstanding calibre and sophistication. Therefore, the main criterion is value for money. A coarsely knotted Mori Bokhara or Indo Mir, for example, can be perfectly acceptable provided that its inferior quality is reflected in the price. More expensive items in the same range should be finely knotted and possess cleanly articulated and symmetrically arranged decorative forms. A useful guide is to apply the following criteria:

    (a) fineness of the knotting
    (b) quality of the materials
    (c) intricacy and symmetrical balance of the design.

Masterworkshop rugs (pls. 38–40) The most prestigious and expensive of all contemporary examples of oriental textile art. The term is often loosely applied to any workshop rug of outstanding calibre, but more specifically refers to items produced in a handful of exceptional workshops in one of the major weaving centres of Persia and Anatolia. There are no hard and fast rules for judging when a workshop qualifies for this accolade, any more than there are for conferring greatness on people and institutions in other forms of art; but it is normally reserved for workshops which consistently produce outstanding items under the direction of a masterweaver, who is accepted by his peers as a pre-eminent exponent of his art.

Consequently, there will always be some debate amongst carpet scholars as to the number and location of masterworkshops at any given time. It is, however, generally accepted that Isfahan, Nain, Hereke, Kashan, Tabriz, Meshed, Kerman and Quoom possess workshops worthy of inclusion in this category. Despite the fact that there are a number of top quality workshops in other countries, none can as yet be considered worthy of a place in the masterworkshop class.

Masterworkshop designs are extremely elaborate and sophisticated interpretations of classical Persian schemes. In addition to opulent versions of the designs associated with their weaving group, most masterworkshops also produce rugs in a number of universal designs, particularly pictorial and garden schemes (pp. 84, 87).

When assessing a masterworkshop rug, look primarily for technical and aesthetic perfection. The knotting should be extremely fine and even throughout; patterns and motifs should be executed with exactness of size and spacing; and the colours should be even and consistent in tone. Flaws are unacceptable, and only the very finest materials should have been used. (*See* p. 22).

A brief history

It is impossible to say with any degree of certainty exactly when, where or by whom the first pile rugs were made. The materials of rug-making are considerably more perishable than those of other types of artefact and consequently very few examples have survived from before the 15th and 16th centuries. The earliest substantial collection of pile fabrics in existence, which dates from between the 5th and 10th centuries AD, was excavated from the burial grounds of Akhmim and Faiÿum in Egypt, and other specimens from the same period have been found throughout Turkey, Central Asia and other parts of the Orient. However, there is a considerable amount of literary and pictorial evidence pointing to the existence of a flourishing tapestry and pile-weaving tradition, stretching from Greece through into Central Asia, which is at least 3,000, and possibly 5,000 years old.

Stone floor panels dating from 883–612 BC, uncovered in the Assyrian royal palaces at Nimrud, Balawat and Nineveh, contain patterns that are generally accepted as carpet designs; there are also a number of reliefs and carvings showing men carrying what can only be tapestries or rugs. Homer, writing c. 900–800 BC, makes frequent reference to 'spreading a rug on a stool' before someone is invited to sit down. He usually employs the word *kivas*, which literally means animal fleece, but occasionally – especially in the scenes where Helen is being entertained – he chooses to use the word *tapés* instead. In the context of the story, Helen, the beautiful and spoilt Princess of Troy, is honoured with a more precious and sophisticated form of seat covering, which given Homer's general description of 'a rug of the softest wool', clearly implies a tapestry or pile rug.

Any lingering doubts as to the existence of rugs in antiquity were dispelled by a remarkable discovery made by the Russian archaeologist S.J. Rundenko during his excavation of a Scythian (or possibly Turkoman) tomb in the Altai mountain range of southern Siberia (1947–49). Among the numerous artefacts uncovered was a miraculously preserved carpet dating from the 5th century BC, which survived because it was frozen in a block of ice after early graverobbers had broken the seal and allowed water into the tomb. The Pazyryk (or Altai) carpet, as it is known, is of crucial importance; not only does it confirm the existence of highly sophisticated hand-knotted rugs during the first millennium BC, it also strengthens the belief that rug-making was widespread throughout the Middle East and Central Asia, because the design is an almost exact replica of one found on a paving slab in the Assyrian royal palace at Nineveh, nearly three thousand miles away.

Most scholars believe that the more advanced civilizations of this era used rugs mainly for decorative purposes – as wall-hangings, bedspreads and covers for seats – and that the use of rugs as floor coverings was evolved by the nomadic tribesmen who ranged the colder, windswept lands of the steppe, tundra and mountain regions of Central Asia. These tribesmen were primarily shepherds who moved with their herds, which were bred for wool as well as meat, in a constant search for good grazing and water. If one excludes cooking utensils, rugs are perhaps the only form of furnishing conducive to this nomadic way of life, because, when spread on the floor, they provide both a comfortable place to sit and a sanitary surface from which to eat food.

Oriental rugs were probably brought into Spain by the Moorish invaders during the 11th and 12th centuries, but it was not until the 14th century that Italian merchants, trading with Anatolia (Turkey) and the Near East, introduced them into most of Europe. The items they brought back were both exotic and expensive, and soon became highly prized by the European aristocracy and wealthier members of the rapidly expanding merchant class. By the 15th century, a steady supply of Anatolian, and perhaps Caucasian and Turkoman rugs were imported by Venetian merchants. It was a source of great prestige to have one's portrait painted while sitting on, or standing near an Anatolian rug, and numerous examples of this can be seen in the pictures of Simone Martini and other artists of the period. This fashion for including rugs in paintings was translated into religious works: Nicholas di Buonaccorsa, Ghirlandaio, Carpaccio and many others depicted the Virgin sitting on a throne with an oriental rug spread out on the floor or steps in front of her. This is, perhaps, the way that the concept of putting rugs on the floor was first introduced into the West; until then, floor coverings had consisted of animal skins, rush matting and, more commonly, loose straw which was frequently changed.

By the late 15th and early 16th centuries the fashion for oriental rugs had spread throughout most of Europe. Henry VIII and Cardinal Wolsey were among the first to import them into England, and the painter Hans Holbein has since had a particular type of design named after him because of the number of times it featured in his portraits of Henry and the English Court. Similarly, the Flemish painter Hans Memlinc provides ample pictorial evidence of the passion for oriental rugs in the Netherlands and Northern Europe.

The magnificent Persian carpets in Western museums, that are generally accepted as being the epitome of oriental textile art, were not made until the early 16th century. Rug-making in Persia took a quantum leap under the patronage of Shah Tamasp (1524–76) and Shah Abbas I (1588–1629); the previous tradition of rather simple geometric designs was superseded by a new-found passion for more naturalistic, usually floral forms in flowing and intricate profusion. Workshops were established in Isfahan, Kashan and Tabriz, and for several decades Persia was the most important and influential centre of artistic excellence and learning in the East – comparable to Renaissance Italy in the West – whose most profound and abiding expression was to be found in the carpets it produced. The effect of these textile masterpieces on European aesthetic tastes was enormous and by the late 17th century few royal houses were without at least one outstanding example of Persian textile art.

They also inspired weavers in Spain, France, Germany, Poland, Ireland, England, Scotland, the Netherlands and much of Northern Europe to create fine carpets of their own. The influence of Anatolian and Persian designs on European compositions is obvious, but each country married this Eastern influence to its own decorative tradition and produced items unique to that country alone. Most Scandinavian rugs, for example, adapted their own folk art traditions; England and Poland incorporated heraldic elements, often reproduced from coats-of-arms, into much more Persian-inspired, Court carpet schemes; France seems to have adopted Eastern weaving techniques but ignored their designs, preferring the more naturalistic floral Aubusson and Savonnerie schemes (p. 85).

By the late 19th century, hand-knotted rugs had almost ceased to be made in Europe, as the advent of weaving machines meant that rugs could be produced much more quickly at a fraction of the cost. The European and American general public of the time were largely unaware of the existence of oriental rugs. This is hardly surprising, for there were very few museums, and the high cost of oriental rugs ensured that they were only affordable by the very rich, who were understandably not inclined to open up their houses to public view. The situation began to change quite rapidly after the Viennese Exhibition of 1873, the first major public exhibition of oriental rugs, and by the turn of this century the interest aroused in Europe and America was such that Persian and Anatolian weavers were prompted to increase production and, in some cases, to modify their designs.

In summary, we can say that rugs were used by a number of civilizations, ranging from Greece through to Central Asia, during the first millennium BC, and were probably in existence for some considerable time before. Certainly, the technique of flatweaving – necessary to make cloth, blankets and *kelims* – can be traced to even older civilizations in the region, and it is anybody's guess as to exactly when and where the notion of introducing a pile into flatwoven material first evolved. The most probable source of this innovation, however, would seem to be the nomadic herdsmen of Central Asia, who possessed both an abundance of rug-making material (i.e., wool provided by their sheep) and the need to combat the harshness of climate and terrain; it is likely that they discovered – possibly by accident – that by looping or knotting short lengths of wool through a flatwoven piece of material they could produce much more comfortable and durable rugs. This technique was then adapted and refined by the more sophisticated cultures of the ancient world, and gradually evolved into what is arguably the most important and universal form of artistic and cultural expression in the East.

Famous carpets and carpet collections

Apart from the Pazyryk carpet (in the Hermitage, Leningrad), probably the most important, and certainly the best known specimen in existence is the Ardebil carpet, which is now housed in London's Victoria and Albert Museum. This masterpiece of oriental textile art, which measures 34′ 6″ × 17′ 6″ (10.52 × 5.33 m) and contains approximately 33 million hand-tied knots at a ratio of 340 knots per in^2, was purchased in about 1880 from a mosque in the north-east Persian town of Ardebil by an English merchant, for approximately £2,400. Today, in the extremely unlikely event of its ever being put up for sale, it would certainly fetch several million US dollars on the open market.

Its design is based around a huge central medallion, encircled by 16 smaller lobe-medallions, set against a field of the most intricately articulated palmettes, floral sprays and *islimi* spirals (pl. 32). It also carries the famous inscription: '*I have no refuge in the world but thy threshold. I have nowhere to hide my head but under this roof. The work is by the slave to the sanctuary. Maksud of Kashan in the year 946.*' (A sister carpet to the Ardebil, which is incomplete because a portion of it was used to repair the one in London, is held in the Los Angeles County Museum of Art.)

Hanging near the Ardebil in the Victoria and Albert Museum is another magnificent 16th-century Persian carpet, known as the Chelsea carpet because it was found in an antique shop in Chelsea, and regarded by many scholars as the most beautiful carpet ever made. An extremely important item, housed in the Österreichisches Museum für Angewandte Kunst in Vienna, is the pure silk Hunting carpet, believed to have been given to Emperor Leopold I by Peter the Great. Equally impressive, and of perhaps even greater historical importance, is the famous Coronation carpet in Rosenborg Castle, Copenhagen. It is knotted in a combination of silk and gold thread, and was reputedly presented to Frederik III's queen, Sophie Amalie, by the Dutch East India Company in 1666. It owes its name to the fact that it was used as the floor covering at the coronation of Frederik IV in 1699, and that of all subsequent absolute kings.

A marvellous stylistic contrast to the intricacy and sophistication of these magnificent Court carpets can be seen in the delightful Marby rug – named after the Swedish village in whose church it was found – which is one of the few remaining examples of the first Anatolian or Caucasian rugs to be brought into the West. Its composition – two pairs of highly stylized facing birds within two large vertically-arranged octagons – is very similar in general character and appearance to the rugs found in such paintings as the *Virgin Enthroned* by Fra Angelico (*c.* 1387–1455) and the *Annunciation* by Carlo Crivelli (*c.* 1430–*c.* 93), and perfectly illustrates the geometric simplicity of this generation of oriental rugs. The Marby rug is now housed in the Statens Historiska Museum in Stockholm, and a very similar item from the same period graces the Berlin Museum.

Public collections of oriental carpets can be found in a number of galleries and museums throughout the Western world; in addition to those already mentioned, the Metropolitan Museum of Art, New York, the Philadelphia Museum of Art and the Poldi Pezzoli Museum, Milan, have carpets that are not to be missed.

Other places with historic oriental carpets are stately homes, churches and public buildings, particularly in Britain and Europe. The list of places with worthwhile examples is far too extensive for inclusion in anything other than a specialist guide to private collections, but a considerable amount of information can be obtained from local tourist authorities and both general and individual heritage guides. It is perhaps more exciting, however, to leave one's discoveries to chance; there can be great satisfaction in wandering round an old country church and suddenly stumbling across an 18th- or 19th-century Persian rug that no one has recognized before.

CHAPTER II

How oriental rugs are made

All oriental rugs are made in one of two ways: they are either hand-woven (*kelims*) or hand-knotted (pile rugs). Individual weaving groups may adopt slightly varying methods of construction, particularly in the type of knot used to form the pile, and it is often these slight differences in weaving and structure, taken in conjunction with their appearance, that enable carpet experts to attribute individual rugs correctly. The fundamentals of construction are basically the same, however, and before discussing the two methods of weaving in detail, it is important to clarify some universal weaving terms.

Warps and wefts

The warp and weft are the basic constituents of all textiles, and are often referred to as the 'foundation' of a rug. The warp describes the strands of material that run lengthways from the top to the bottom of a rug and form the fringes at the ends; the weft runs widthways and forms the selvedges, or sides. Normally both the warp and the weft are made from the same material, but it is not unknown, particularly in village and nomadic rugs, for contrasting materials to be used – a woollen warp may be used in conjunction with a cotton weft, for example.

Selvedges and fringes

The selvedges are the outer edges of the rug where the weft strands have been wrapped around the last few warp strands in order to hold the rug tightly together across its width. The fringes are continuations of the warp strands, and are secured at the top and bottom of the rug to both hold the weft strands in place and add the final decorative touch to the rug.

Selvedges are more or less the same on all items, but the fringes are secured in a number of distinctive ways.

Tied fringe Probably the most common and found in rugs from a broad cross-section of weaving groups. Two or more warp strands are tied together to form a knot which presses against the final weft strand and holds it in place. The process is repeated across the entire width of the rug.

Kelim (or Plaited) fringe The weft strands are continued beyond the edge of the pile and interwoven with the warp strands to form a short length of *kelim* at either end of the rug. This method is also extremely common. (*See* pl. 10).

Woven fringe A narrow strip of pile material is added to a *kelim* fringe. It may be continuous or broken into segments, and usually runs along the top and bottom fringes approximately mid-way between the end of the fringe and the beginning of the main body of the rug. Woven fringes are usually found only in workshop and master-workshop rugs.

Looms

Weaving looms differ considerably in size and sophistication, but all operate on exactly the same principle, which requires a secure frame on which to tie the warp strands. This is achieved by constructing a rectangular framework, usually of wood, which may be either of fixed dimensions or adjustable in size. On fixed frames, the weaver can only make rugs in sizes smaller than the inner dimensions of the frame; adjustable frames allow one or more of the beams to be extended so that larger items can be woven. On most adjustable looms the vertical beams are fixed and one or both of the horizontal beams, which hold the warp strands in place, can be moved up or down the frame. Needless to say, the type of loom used is a crucial factor determining the size and structural quality of the rugs woven by each weaving group.

Horizontal (or Nomadic) looms The most simple and primitive in contemporary use, these looms have changed little since their inception several millennia ago; they consist of four wooden beams which are laid out flat and secured by pegs driven into the ground. As the name implies, they are used almost exclusively by nomadic weavers. The fact that the loom is horizontal means that the women have to do much of their weaving from the sides, which becomes impossible if the rugs are too wide; consequently, nomadic rugs tend to be either small, or long and narrow. Having to work from different angles makes it extremely difficult to maintain an even symmetry throughout the design, and it is therefore not surprising that nomadic rugs sometimes contain motifs of slightly varying sizes; the fact that so many are perfectly balanced and symmetrical is a glowing testament to the weavers' skill. Despite the limitations of the horizontal loom, it is eminently suited to the nomads' way of life, being both easy to assemble and take down, and not too large or cumbersome to be carried by donkey or camel.

Village loom Only slightly more sophisticated than nomadic looms, these are constructed from two vertical beams, either driven into the ground or secured on a stable base, with two horizontal beams fastened at the top and the bottom of the uprights. Because they are vertical these looms allow the weaver easy access to every point across the width of the rug, and it is possible to produce much wider rugs. However, the overall size of rugs that can be made is restricted by the fixed beams, and village weavers rarely produce large carpets.

Adjustable looms Some village and workshop groups use looms with horizontal beams which can be adjusted to alter the length of the rug. A more sophisticated version of this type is the Tabriz loom, used primarily by workshop groups. It was developed specifically for the larger urban workshops and consists of an adjustable loom with a device which, by altering the tension on the warp strands, shifts the completed work to the rear of the loom, allowing the weaver to sit at the same level through-out the entire rug-making process. This innovation makes it possible to produce rugs that are almost twice as long as the distance between the horizontal beams.

Roller looms take the weaving process one step further with a development which is simplicity itself. The warp strands are fed individually to the horizontal beam at the bottom of the loom which can be rotated so that the finished portions of the rug are rolled onto the beam. Its advantage over the Tabriz loom is that even larger carpets can be made. These two types are now standard equipment in workshops and master-workshops throughout the weaving world.

Tools

Weaving tools consist of a knife, a beating comb and shears. These may vary a little in size and construction, and individual weavers may have several slightly different versions of each, but they are always basically the same.

Knife Used to cut the threads of the pile and foundation material; it usually has a hook on the end of the blade to assist in the formation of the knot.

A non-adjustable village loom.

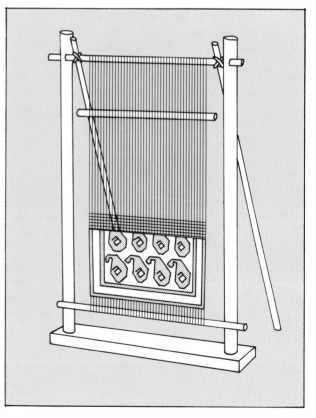

Beating comb Consists of a series of metal blades which are splayed to form a set of sharp teeth. It is used to tighten (or beat) the threads of the weft against the line of knots tied around the warp strings, ensuring the compactness of the rug.

Shears Used to clip the pile to an even level once the weaving has been completed.

Materials

Oriental rugs always use natural fibres, and any rug containing synthetic material will invariably have been machine made. The only exception to this rule is the occasional use of very small quantities of gold or metallic thread in some workshop and masterworkshop items. Wool, cotton and silk are the main materials, although goat and camel hair are sometimes used by nomadic and village weavers.

Wool The best and most widely used rug-making material. It is soft, durable and easy to work. However, the quality varies considerably and not all wool is suitable for rug-making. Good carpet wool needs to combine softness with strength and springiness, otherwise the rug wears out quickly and fails to return to its original shape if creased or depressed. Only certain types of wool possess the qualities required; the best comes from lambs between 8 and 14 months old, particularly those from the colder highland regions. Unless one has followed the rug-making process through from clipping to completion, the only way to assess the quality of the wool is to rely on the 'feel' of the item and the reputation of the individual weaving group. However, some rugs are prefixed by the word Kurk (or Kork) – as in Kurk Kashan – which indicates that the rug was made from wool taken from the flanks and shoulders – where the fibres are longest – of lambs reared in the winter and clipped in the spring. Kurk wool is generally considered to be among the very best available.

The process of turning freshly shorn wool into yarn suitable for rug-making is both simple and universal. The wool is first washed – normally after shearing – and then 'carded', a process that teases the wool into longer and straighter fibres. The fibres are then spun, either by hand or machine, into a continuous thread which is twisted together with other threads, in the opposite direction to which they were spun, to form the yarn. The individual threads are referred to as 'ply', and the more that go into making a yarn, the thicker and stronger it will be.

As a general rule, the wool in nomadic items is very good. Equally, that found in Persian and Afghan rugs is of high quality. Chinese wool is also excellent, but wool from India and Pakistan, although often beautifully lustrous, is a little too soft for rug-making. (Superior quality Australian, New Zealand and Belouch wool is often used in the better items, however.) Anatolian rugs have improved considerably in recent years, and the general quality of their wool is good. As a foundation material it is only used by nomadic and some village weavers. It has a tendency to lose its shape and can only be spun into relatively thick strands. This can add a degree of primitive charm to tribal rugs, however.

Cotton Normally only used for foundations. (The main exception to this rule is Kayseria, in Anatolia, which produces rugs with mercerized cotton piles normally marketed as 'art' silk.) Cotton is grown in most rug-making countries in the East – particularly in India and Persia – and is consequently in plentiful supply. As a foundation material it has numerous advantages: it is strong, does not lose its shape and can be spun into strands sufficiently thin to allow fine weaving. It is, however, susceptible to mildew.

Silk Produced by the larva of a species of moth (*bombix mori*) commonly called the silkworm. It is native to China and has been cultivated successfully in a number of countries, including Iran, Turkey, India and the Soviet Union. The finest silk for rug-making traditionally comes from China and an area around the Caspian Sea. This latter region produces a type referred to as *rasht* silk, which is generally regarded as the best in the world.

Silk is used either on its own or in combination with wool by a number of individual weaving groups in all the major rug-making countries, with the exception of the Soviet Union, the Balkans and Pakistan, where very few silk or part-silk items are produced. Silk has a number of limitations. It is reasonably hardwearing but it lacks the springiness and suppleness of wool; consequently, silk rugs tend to retain any creases or scuffing in the pile, and far greater care is needed to protect them from damage. It is also extremely expensive, and only the most profligate would consider using a pure silk rug as a functional floor covering. However, its physical beauty is unsurpassed and silk rugs are normally used as decorative, rather than functional examples of textile art – either as wall-hangings, or floor coverings in rooms that rarely see practical use. Silk is also used as a foundation material; it is extremely strong, keeps its shape, and can be spun into very fine strands, but because of its cost it is only used when exceptionally fine knotting is required.

Dyeing and colours

The dyer is an extremely important, and often somewhat mysterious figure in rug-making. In nomadic and village cultures, the master dyer – almost invariably male – often acts as the tribal wise man, whose advice is sought on a whole range of subjects that have nothing to do with making rugs. Dyeing is considered a science, whose secrets are handed down from generation to generation, and when the dyer is working, only other dyers may speak to him. This mystique is understandably less pronounced in modern urban manufactories, but the dyer is nevertheless a figure of considerable importance and prestige.

Dyeing begins after the wool has been cleaned, usually by washing in a weak solution of soda and soap, when it is immersed in an alum-bath for about 12 hours. The alum acts as a mordant (a chemical used to create a bond between the fibre and the dyestuff), and after the yarn has been satisfactorily treated it is soaked in a bath of dye. Between each stage the yarn is left out in the sun to dry.

Natural dyes Often referred to as vegetable dyes, despite the fact that many of them are obtained from animal and mineral sources. Although the majority of weaving groups today use chemical dyes, they are still used by a number of nomadic and village groups. In fact, the Turkish government has recently encouraged their use, and a growing number of Anatolian weaving groups are now returning to these traditional dyes, in spite of the fact that good quality synthetic dyes are reasonably cheap and plentiful. This reflects both a desire to uphold tradition and the fact that natural dyes produce a subtle beauty of tone that has never been equalled by even the finest synthetic dyes.

The natural dyestuffs have the advantage of being readily found in the natural environment. Red is obtained from the roots of the madder plant (*rubia tinctorum*) and also from the crushed bodies of female insects of the *coccus cacti* genus, which produce a colour usually referred to as cochineal or carmine red. A third shade of red is derived from the insect *chermes abietis*. Yellow is made from the reseda plant, vine leaves and pomegranate skins. Saffron yellow comes from the dried pistils of the saffron crocus, but this plant is now extremely rare and the colour is exceptionally expensive. Blue is derived from the ubiquitous indigo plant, and green is produced by mixing yellow and blue. Grey and brown are obtained either by using undyed wool or by dyeing the yarns with extracts from nutshells and oak bark.

Chemical dyes These were introduced into Persia and Anatolia in the late 19th century, but proved to be totally unsuitable for rug yarns, producing rather crude colours that were given to rapid fading. In 1903 the Persian government stopped the import of these aniline dyes and brought in laws, which were strictly enforced, ordering dye-houses found using them to be burnt to the ground. In addition, any weaver caught using illegally dyed yarns could be sentenced to having his right arm cut off. Needless to say, these measures proved effective, and Persian weavers went back to using natural dyes until the more reliable chrome dyes were introduced in the years between the First and Second World Wars.

(Aniline dyes were not banned in Anatolia, and their use helps to explain why Anatolian rugs of this period are generally considered inferior to those produced today.) Modern chrome dyes are, however, extremely reliable, colour-fast and made in a wide range of attractive colours and shades. Today's buyer can be assured that the colours, whether from natural or synthetic dyes, will only improve with age.

Abrash Name given to a sudden change in the intensity or tone of a particular colour which does not correspond to any similar change in design. It is caused by the weaver moving to a separately dyed batch of yarn part-way through making a rug. Abrashes are usually found in nomadic and village items, where only small amounts of yarn can be dyed at any one time, and are not a sign of inadequate craftsmanship. However, they are not acceptable in workshop items.

The relationship between colour and age As a rug begins to age its colours lose some of their intensity and the sharp divisions of tone gradually mellow into a more harmonious whole. This process may take 20 years or more to complete, and is more pronounced if natural dyes have been used or if the rug has been exposed to direct sunlight. It is an important factor in dating a rug (p. 33).

The meaning of individual colours Varies from culture to culture. In Muslim countries, green – the colour of Mohammed's coat – is sacred and is very rarely used as a predominant colour; but it forms an important part of the dyer's palette in non-Muslim cultures, particularly China; here, the sacred colour is yellow, in which the Emperor traditionally dressed. White represents grief to the Chinese, Indians and Persians. Blue symbolizes heaven in Persia, and power and authority in Mongolia. Orange is synonymous with piety and devotion in Muslim countries, while red, the most universal rug colour, is widely accepted as a sign of wealth and rejoicing.

Flatweaves, or kelims

Flatwoven rugs are generally referred to as *kelims* (or *gelims*), which is a Turkish word meaning prayer rug. They are made by tightly interweaving the warp and weft strands to create a flat, pileless surface. The design is produced by threading the weft strands through a number of the warp strands, rather than directly from edge to edge, and then looping them back around the last warp thread used. Each section of the overall design is woven separately, and when one part of the pattern is completed a new, usually different-coloured, weft thread is inserted at the point where the last one finished. The angular nature of most patterns allows the warp strands to be overlapped by two or more sections of the wefted pattern, ensuring that the rug is bonded firmly across the width. On the rare occasions when vertical stripes are used in the design, the adjoining sections are either stitched together at the back, or the first and last weft threads from the adjoining segments of pattern are tied around the same warp strand – a technique used by the American Indians in weaving blankets. Consequently, the weft strands form the pattern on the face of the rug which, because they have been looped back around the warp strands, is clearly visible from both back and front.

Kelims are much quicker and cheaper to produce than pile rugs, and this is normally reflected in their price. However, they have become increasingly collectable in recent years and are no longer as inexpensive as they were. (*See* pl. 23).

Tapestry weaving A very similar technique to *kelim* weaving. It can be easily distinguished because the weft strands are left hanging at the back, and the design can only be seen from the front.

Soumak technique Associated with the Caucasian weaving group of the same name which has produced this highly distinctive type of flatwoven rug for generations. The design is created by wrapping a weft thread around four (or sometimes more) warp strands and then drawing it back and wrapping it around two, a technique of 'looped' weaving not dissimilar to the way fishermen make their nets. It produces a slight herringbone effect on the face of the rug and a series of ridges along the back. The easiest

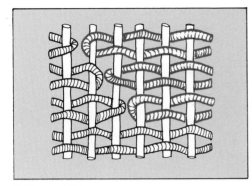

Kelim weaving.

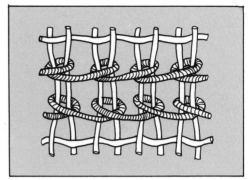

Soumak weaving.

way to recognize Soumak weaving is to turn the item over and note the unclipped strands of weft hanging from the back.

Dhurries and druggets Not generally classified as oriental rugs, despite being made in the Orient. Dhurries are flatwoven rugs made in India using the warp-sharing technique (i.e., looping two separate parts of the wefted pattern around the same warp). They usually employ simple geometric designs and are very cheap. Druggets are made in India and the Balkan countries, usually from a combination of goat hair, cotton and jute, and are equally cheap and cheerful, but not so frequently found. These comments only apply to modern dhurries and druggets; older items have become quite collectable in recent years.

Knotted, or pile rugs

In oriental rugs the pile is created by tying a short length of yarn around two adjacent warp strands so that the ends of the yarn protrude upwards to form the surface (or pile) of the rug. This process is referred to as 'knotting', because when the weft and warp strands are beaten together to hold the yarn in place, a securely tied knot is formed. In oriental rugs, every knot – which corresponds to two individual strands of pile – is tied by hand, and a skilled weaver can tie something in the region of a thousand knots per hour. The knotting process always begins at the side of the rug (after the selvedges have been secured) by tying a knot on each pair of warp strands in a horizontal direction across the width of the rug. When one horizontal line of knots has been tied, they are beaten tightly together with the weaver's comb before starting on the next line, and this continues upwards until the rug has been completed.

Different types of knot

There are two main types of knot used in contemporary oriental weaving: the Senneh (or Persian) knot and the Ghiordes (or Turkish) knot. Each has its own slight advantages and disadvantages, but, in practice, both are excellent for the purpose, and the choice of knot does not affect the overall quality of the rug. However, knowing which type of knot has been used is extremely important in helping to determine where a particular rug was made, because although individual weaving groups may copy each other's designs, they rarely, if ever, change the knot they use.

Senneh or Persian knot Formed by looping the pile yarn through two warp strands and then drawing it back through one. It is also referred to as the 'asymmetrical' knot because the pile yarn may be drawn to either the right or the left of the warp strands. Many experts argue that the Persian knot makes it easier to produce intricate, curvilinear designs by enabling the weaver to tie more knots to the square inch, but this theory is by no means universally accepted in the carpet trade. The Persian knot is used almost exclusively in China, India, Pakistan and the Balkan countries. It is also widely used

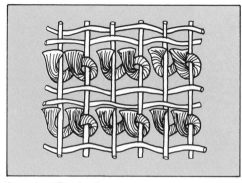

Senneh or Persian knot.

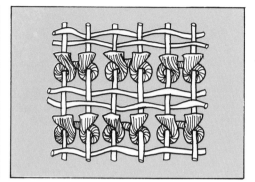

Ghiordes or Turkish knot.

throughout Persia and Afghanistan – although, ironically, not in the Persian town of Senneh from which it derived its name. A simple, though far from foolproof, method of telling whether the Senneh knot has been used is to examine the back of the rug. Usually, if only one loop or bump is visible across the warp where the knot has been tied, then the Persian knot has been employed.

Ghiordes or Turkish knot Formed by looping the pile yarn across two warp strands and then drawing each end back through the inside of both warps. This 'symmetrical knot', as it is often called, produces extremely compact rugs. It is used almost exclusively by Caucasian and Anatolian weaving groups and also by several in Persia, particularly in the north-west of the country. There is no foolproof way of determining if a Turkish knot has been used, but a fair indication can be obtained by looking at the back of the rug. If two loops or bumps are visible across the warp on which the knot has been tied, the Turkish knot has probably been employed.

Jufti knot Vastly inferior knot produced by tying the pile yarn around four or more warp strands, rather than the customary two. This increases the speed at which a rug can be woven but results in its being less compact and durable. Use of the jufti knot was rife in Persia in the first half of this century, but the practice is less common in contemporary rugs. However, some items, particularly from Persia and Pakistan, are still made with it. These are usually otherwise quite finely woven workshop rugs in

which the weaver, to save time and money, has employed jufti knots on the single-coloured, unpatterned areas where a high knot-count is not necessary to articulate the design. A simple method of telling whether a jufti knot has been used is to compare the horizontal knot-count to the number of warps. If there are more than twice as many warps as there are knots, then the jufti knot has almost certainly been employed.

Fineness of the knotting

This refers to the number of knots that have been tied per in^2 of pile. The higher the number of knots, the finer the weave. There are no hard and fast rules determining the exact knot-count required to justify a rug being referred to as 'fine' or 'finely knotted', but anything over c. 150 knots per in^2 can be considered medium grade (reasonably finely knotted) and anything over 250 or 300 would generally be acknowledged as top grade (fine).

The fineness of the knotting is not an infallible indicator of quality. If very thick yarns are used, as they are in Chinese and other good quality items, the number of knots that can be tied per in^2 is understandably less than if thinner yarns are employed. Equally, regularity and evenness of knotting are crucial to the structural and compositional integrity of a rug: the knot-count should be the same throughout the entire rug and the rows straight and uniformly spaced. However, a high knot-count is necessary to produce extremely intricate designs and the more intricate the design, the more knots needed to ensure its success.

This is particularly true when articulating curved or flowing forms.

To determine the fineness of the knotting, count the number of individual knots that occupy a linear inch on both the horizontal and vertical axes of any part of the rug, and then multiply the two numbers together. Measurements may be calculated in square feet, centimetres or millimetres, but the square inch (in^2) and square metre (m^2) are by far the most commonly used, and will be employed throughout the following chapters.

Another common way of measuring the fineness of the knotting is to count the number of knots running widthways along a linear foot across the rug. This is referred to as a 'line', and is the standard measurement used in Chinese carpets – for example, a '90-line' carpet will have 90 knots per linear foot along each horizontal row.

Pakistani weavers have their own unique way of measuring the fineness of their rugs. As they use much thinner weft than warp strands, more knots are tied on the vertical than the horizontal axis. The fineness of Pakistani rugs is therefore graded as 10/20 or 12/24, etc., with the first figure referring to the number of knots running per linear inch along the horizontal axis, and the second figure to the number running the same distance along the vertical. A 10/20 Pakistani rug is therefore equivalent in fineness to a 200 per in^2 Persian rug.

Clipping

Once a rug has been completed and taken off the loom, the pile is clipped to its required length. A preliminary clipping usually takes place during the course of the knotting, when the weaver cuts the pile yarn to an approximate length after he or she has completed a few rows, but the final clipping is a highly skilled job, which, if badly done, can ruin months of work. Amongst nomadic and village groups the final shearing is often done by the weaver, but in workshops a specialist is normally employed. The length of pile after clipping is largely determined by the stylistic traditions of the particular weaving group or by the market at which the rug is aimed. Some groups have always produced rugs with close-cropped piles,

while others seem to prefer longer, more fleecy items. The only other external modifying force is the fact that extremely intricate designs tend to become unclear if the pile is too long, which is why most finely-knotted items are close-cropped.

Embossing or incising Common in most Chinese and some Indian and Anatolian rugs, this entails cutting an angular groove in the pile around certain motifs to create a relief effect which accentuates elements of the design. This technique can only be applied in bold, relatively thick outlines, and is therefore only used on items which employ reasonably simple designs. In more intricate rugs this accentuating process is normally achieved by outlining the motifs in a different material, usually silk.

Washing

After the rug has been clipped, it is washed to remove any dirt that may have been collected during the weaving process and to give the pile its particular 'finish'. Sometimes the rug is simply washed in water and then left out in the sun to dry, but many weaving groups now add chemicals to the water in order both to alter the tonal intensity of the colours and to give the pile a gloss or matt sheen. Light chemical washes simply take the edge off the harsher colours, reproducing a degree of the tonal mellowness that comes with age, and have only a minimal effect on the integrity of the pile. Heavy chemical washes, however, particularly those which dramatically reduce the tonal intensity of the colours or introduce a high-gloss sheen, can seriously weaken the fabric and undermine the durability of the rug. There are several different washes currently in use, but the most common are:

Gold washing Used to bleach out the red tones. This process can sometimes weaken the pile fibres, but it produces extremely attractive shades of muted red and rose.

Sun washing Refers to rugs left in the sun until their colours are bleached to more mellow shades. This term is now commonly applied to a number of items, particularly from Anatolia, which have light pastel shades. However, this 'sun-washed' effect, which emulates the ageing process, is often achieved by chemical washing, and it is advisable not to take the term too literally. A simple way to tell whether an item has been sun washed or chemically washed is to open the pile. If the colours are lighter near the surface, the chances are that it is either old or has genuinely been bleached by the sun. In practice, only *kelims* are usually finished in this way.

Lustre washing Gives the pile a glossy, silken appearance, which can be extremely visually appealing. It is most widely used in Pakistan, and all but the poorest quality Mori Bokharas are normally given a lustre wash. Dealers often tell potential customers that the rug's silken appearance is due to the superb quality of the wool. This is nonsense; the lustre is solely the result of the chemical washing.

Antique finishing The term given to a chemical wash that reproduces the effects of age. It is normally used on a range of Chinese rugs which employ the more traditional designs, and can sometimes be so authentic in appearance that experts have been fooled.

Painted rug One which has been dyed on the surface after the weaving has been completed. This technique was developed to intensify certain colours which could not be produced in deep enough shades in the yarn, and was often used on items from the Arak region of Persia, particularly on Lilihan Sarouks. Today this method is in decline.

Sizes and shapes

In the East it is customary to employ several rugs in an overall floor plan, rather than opting for one large, centralized carpet as in the West. This has a number of practical advantages from a furnishing and decorative point of view. If the owner moves to

A traditional arrangement of Persian rugs. *Above and centre*: the 'lightning' design found in Hamadan rugs. *Left and right*: repeating amulet/medallion designs.

larger or smaller premises, rugs can simply be added or taken away; equally, if a rug is damaged another can be purchased for far less than it would cost to have the entire floor covering replaced; and by simply interchanging items it is also possible to alter the whole appearance of a room. It is perhaps for these entirely practical reasons that each approximate size and shape of rug is known by a specific name which usually relates either to its traditional position on the floor or the purpose for which it was made.

How rugs are measured depends on the individual country. Linear measurements may be given either in imperial or metric units, but area is normally quoted in square metres. The following list is given in descending order of size.

Qali Persian word, which literally means carpet, applied to any large item measuring over 10′ × 6′ (3.05 × 1.83 m).

Kellegi From the Persian word *kelley* (head), it is applied to the main or 'head' carpet in the traditional arrangement. It is usually 2 or 3 times longer than it is wide, and can measure anything from 12′ to 24′ long and 6′ to 8′ wide (3.66/7.32 × 1.83/2.44 m).

Kenareh Derived from the Persian word *kenar* (side), it is the side carpet in the traditional arrangement. It is a narrower version of a *kellegi* and is usually between 10′ and 24′ long by 3′ to 5′ wide (3.05/7.32 × 0.91/1.52 m).

Dozar Literally means two *zars* – a *zar* being a Persian unit of measurement of c. 4′ 2″ (1.28 m). The term is applied to rugs which are about 8′ (or two *zars*) in length and 5′/6′ wide (2.44 × 1.52/1.83 m).

Sedjadeh and khalichen Alternative, though far less common terms for rugs of *dozar* size. The term *khalichen* is usually reserved for very high quality items made in these dimensions.

Zaronim Derived from two Persian words – *zar* and *nim* (half) – it literally means one and a half *zars*. In practice, a *zaronim* is usually around 6′ by 4′ (1.83 × 1.22 m) or 5′ by 3′ 6″ (1.52 × 1.07 m).

Seccade Turkish term for rugs c. 6′ 6″ by 3′ 9″ (1.98 × 1.14 m). This size is frequently encountered in contemporary Anatolian village rugs.

Pushti and yastik Persian and Turkish terms respectively (meaning cushion), applied to small bedside rugs of about 3′ by 2′ (0.91 × 0.61 m).

Ceyrek Name given to Anatolian rugs measuring c. 4′ 6″ by 2′ 9″ (1.37 × 0.84 m).

Rugs for special purposes

Prayer rug Name given to the small rug which Muslims kneel upon when praying. The term is also used to describe a general design (p. 85).

Saph Term used for a multiple prayer rug – one with two or more separate prayer fields – which is also referred to as a family prayer rug (p. 86).

Enessi or Enssi A rug which is used as a door or curtain at the entrance of a Turkoman tent. It is also more generally applied to the *hatchli* design (p. 91).

Other textile artefacts

In addition to rugs there are a number of extremely attractive and collectable items that also have specific names. For the most part they comprise various types of bag, hangings and camel- or donkey-trappings made by nomadic and semi-nomadic tribesmen for their own personal use.

Juval Turkish term for a camel bag or bagface measuring c. 6′ × 3′ (1.83 × 0.91 m).

Torba Turkoman storage bag, usually measuring c. 4′ × 2′ 6″ (1.22 × 0.76 m).

Churdjin or Khordjin Small saddle bags, for donkeys.

Mafrash Large saddle bags.

Tschoval Storage bag, usually larger than a *torba*.

Hehbelyk General name for a saddle cover.

Tsherlik Small saddle cover.

Asmalyk Turkoman term for the twin flank trappings used to adorn wedding camels.

Turbehlyk A grave rug.

CHAPTER III

Buying a rug

Choosing an oriental rug

The most important factor when choosing an oriental rug is the reason 'why' the rug is being bought. This may seem self-evident, but it is not unknown for people to purchase extremely attractive and reasonably priced items only to find, when they take them home, that they are the wrong size, or that the colour and design clash with their decorative scheme. Equally, some rugs which represent extremely good value as furnishing items, are not suitable for long-term investments, while rugs with the highest investment potential may be out of place as decorative items in the home. Some rugs are also more durable than others, and you should remember to take this into account when choosing the type most suited to each room or function.

Decorative considerations

The vast majority of people buy oriental rugs in order to enhance the decorative integrity of their homes. They are not concerned with investment potential or collectability, and the fact that items may appreciate in value over the years is a bonus, rather than the main reason for which they are bought. Consequently, the prime considerations are colour, design and size.

Colour
Today, rugs are an important export for most producing countries, and many weaving groups have consciously broadened their palette in order to appeal to Western tastes. This is particularly true of India and Pakistan, where traditional Persian and Turkoman designs are now produced in a range of pastel shades. Chinese rugs have long been in tune with Western colour schemes, and a growing number of Anatolian groups are now producing traditional and Caucasian designs in much softer shades. In contrast, most nomadic and tribal groups still make rugs in the time-honoured dark reds and primary hues of their ancestors, while Persian workshop groups employ both pastel and rich shades. Almost every design is now available in the widest possible variety of tonal schemes,
and the prospective buyer should have no problem in finding a rug to suit the other furnishings in his or her home.

Both harmonious and contrasting shades can be used to enhance the decorative impact of a room. For a harmonious effect, aim to reflect the overall tonality of the room, or ensure that a single colour from the woodwork or furnishings is echoed in the rug. This does not have to be the most dominant colour in either the room or the rug; better results are often achieved by matching subsidiary colours, provided they are not swamped by other shades: for example, a predominantly red rug with strong hints of blue can blend well into a room with some blues but no reds.

Contrasting shades can enliven a room by providing an invigorating tonal counterpoint, but care needs to be taken to ensure that colours do not clash. This is less of a danger if the room is decorated in neutral shades, or if the rug's colours are echoed in the other furnishings; for example, a room with some pastel blues or reds can be wonderfully enlivened by introducing a rug with much richer shades of blue or red. *Pastel shades* are extremely versatile and blend with most traditional Western furnishings and interior designs. *Strong or dark shades* are normally only found in nomadic and tribal rugs. They are particularly suitable for the rough-hewn surroundings of old country cottages, but can also be ideal for studies, dens, and rooms where the dominant colours are neutral or autumnal browns. *Rich shades* are perfectly in tune with opulent surroundings, but can also enhance a pastel decor.

Design

In many ways, design is less critical than colour, as the colour of a rug has far more impact on its surroundings; a discordant pattern will still blend into most rooms, providing the colours are harmonious. However, choosing the right design is important in reinforcing the style and decorative atmosphere of a room.

Curvilinear designs Usually rather intricate and floral-inspired, they find their best expression in classically furnished rooms; the more ornate and intricately decorated the surroundings, the more a curvilinear rug will enhance the effect. This type of design can also add a degree of opulence to a plainly decorated room, but careful consideration is necessary before placing a curvilinear design rug in a room with rustic or Scandinavian-type furnishings, as the two styles may clash.

Geometric designs Particularly compatible with Scandinavian and Bauhaus-inspired designs. They can also look good in more classically furnished rooms, provided the tonality of the rug matches the general decor.

Repeating designs Employ a single motif, or group of motifs repeated throughout the rug (*herati*, *boteh*, etc.). The pattern is the same from every angle, which affords considerable freedom in the placement of the rug. This is crucial in the successful location of runners and room-size carpets.

Centralized designs Employ a single centralized motif – usually a medallion – and rely for their success on the balance between the focal motif and the surrounding design. This symmetry can be disturbed if one side of the rug is disproportionately near a wall or piece of furniture, and they should ideally be placed in a central position. If this is not possible, allow roughly the same amount of space on each opposing side (for example, by placing one side of the rug a few feet from a wall and the opposite side the same distance from a large piece of furniture). This is generally more critical with larger items.

Vertical and horizontal designs The design runs one way along the rug, and needs to be seen from a particular angle for maximum effect. This is essential with prayer rugs and pictorial carpets, which lose much of their impact if viewed upside-down. Finding the optimum location is largely a matter of trial and error, but aim to place them where they cannot be seen upside-down (i.e., with the top end facing a wall), or use them as wall-hangings.

For more information on the designs mentioned here, refer to Chapter IV.

Size

Choosing the correct size is not as simple as merely ensuring that the rug fits into the appropriate space. Oriental rugs need room to breathe, and unless they are given the right amount of space they can either be swamped by the surrounding decor or become so overpowering that they detract from everything else in the room. The amount of space necessary depends on both the decor and furnishings, and the strength of colour and pattern in the rug. Boldly patterned and strongly coloured rugs need more space than those with more delicate compositions and pastel shades. Much also depends on the amount of furniture in the room; the less furniture, the more space that can be occupied by the rug without the room appearing too cluttered.

Assessing quality

Contrary to popular myth, assessing quality is not as difficult as it might first appear; armed with a little basic information, anyone should be able to distinguish a good from a poor quality rug. Obviously, there is some truth in the old maxim that 'you get what you pay for', but as in many other areas of life, price and value are not always synonymous, and you should be very wary of accepting without question that something is necessarily better because it costs more.

Quality is determined by a combination of aesthetic and structural considerations. The former cannot be defined by any objective criteria and are largely a matter of personal taste, although if you wish to guarantee a reasonable resale value, it is crucial to make sure that your tastes coincide with more universally held views on aesthetic appeal. Therefore, apply the criteria for each weaving category (p. 11) and take into account any characteristics associated with each specific weaving group (Chs. VI, VII). Structural quality can be assessed far more objectively. There are four main points to consider:

(a) the fineness and regularity of the knotting;
(b) the clarity and permanence of the dyes;
(c) the suitability of the pile material; and
(d) whether the rug lies evenly on the floor.

Remember that some criteria are more applicable to certain categories of rug than to others; for example, the fineness of the knotting is more critical in workshop rugs than it is in village or nomadic items. Always use the appropriate yardstick for each category. However, the same criteria should be applied to all rugs when assessing the suitability of the pile material and the clarity and permanence of the dyes, as there is no uniform improvement in the quality of these as items move up the price range from nomadic to masterworkshop.

The first step in assessing quality Look at the back of the rug. This is necessary not only to judge the fineness and regularity of the knotting, but also to discover whether there are any repairs or signs of damage which are not noticeable from the front. On a good rug, the design should be clearly visible on the back, and it is often easier, particularly in long-pile carpets, to see any faults in the symmetry or articulation of the motifs.

Estimating the fineness of the knotting Turn the rug over so that the pile is facing the floor and then calculate the knot-count as outlined in Chapter II (p. 27). The knots running crossways form small ridges on the warp strands, which makes them easy to count, and those running lengthways correspond to each individual weft yarn. If you experience difficulty in picking out the individual knots, use a magnifying glass. Alternatively, a fairly shrewd idea can be obtained by simply looking at the back. If the design appears clear and even throughout, and the foundation strands form a neat grid, then the knotting is almost certainly regular. If the spacing between the strands is uneven, or if they curve or go off at an angle, the knotting is irregular, and denotes a poor quality rug.

Similarly, the fineness of the knotting can be judged by standing as far away from the rug as is necessary before the individual knots merge into the overall design. It is like viewing an Impressionist painting, where the viewer is required to stand at a certain distance before the image comes into focus; the bigger the individual strokes of paint, the further back the viewer has to stand. Similarly, the finer the knotting in an oriental rug, the closer one can get before the individual knots begin to show.

Quality of the dyes This can only be properly tested in a laboratory, but all dyes used today are both permanent and colour-fast. Provided the colours look attractive when the rug is purchased, the overwhelming probability is that they will only improve with age.

Suitability of the pile material Materials vary from weaving group to weaving group, and occasionally between different items produced by the same group. More detailed information on the quality of the pile materials used by individual countries and weaving groups is contained in Chapters V, VI and VII. A simple test for woollen rugs is to fold or crease the pile and see how quickly the wool returns to its original shape. If it does not crease easily, or if the pile returns to its former shape when smoothed out flat, the wool is probably good. If the rug retains the creases, or if they prove difficult to dislodge, then the wool is too soft and inelastic for top quality pile material. This test should never be applied to silk rugs, as creasing can damage the fibres. Look instead for a degree of suppleness in the fabric and the extent to which the colours alter their intensity when viewed from different angles; the more readily they submit to subtle changes in the direction of the light source, the more likely it is that good quality silk has been used.

To test whether a rug lies flat Always lay the rug on a flat and even surface, and after smoothing it out, carefully view it from all sides to see if there are any ridges or troughs. Repeat the viewing process after walking across the rug a few times, as this will show how it responds to use. Then run your hand across the surface in order to detect any bumps or depressions not visible to the eye. A certain degree of unevenness is acceptable in nomadic and some village items.

Dating

Discovering exactly when an undated rug was made is almost impossible. However, complete accuracy is not important, as a few years either way make little difference to its value or collectability; placing it in the right quarter of the appropriate century will nearly always suffice. The one exception is when an item is on the borderline between being old and antique. (The definition of antique varies between '100 years old' and 'made before the turn of the century'.) Accurate dating is crucial in these cases because tax regulations in some countries provide exemptions for antiques; these vary from country to country, and advice should be taken locally.

Establishing when a rug was made This is achieved by carefully examining its structure and design, which usually change to some degree with time, and taking into account its general condition and appearance. Dating a rug from its weave and design requires extensive specialist knowledge and can only be undertaken by an expert. The condition and appearance of a rug can be affected by a number of factors other than age, and it is dangerous to jump to the conclusion that something is necessarily old because it is worn and in a poor state of repair. A relatively old rug that has been well looked after may be in far better condition than a newer item that has seen less considerate use, and some contemporary items are deliberately made to look old by the use of chemical washes (p. 27).

A more reliable determinant of age is the way the colours have changed (p. 24). As a rug gets older the colours become more subdued; this mellowing process is caused by the reaction of the dyes to light, and it can take between 20 and 50 years before the rug reaches what is generally referred to as 'the primary stage of mellowness'. By looking into the pile of a rug and comparing the intensity of colours with those on the surface, you can obtain a rough idea of how far the mellowing process has progressed. This is not an exact method as the rate of fading is determined by the length of time a rug has been exposed to the light and by the intensity of the light source. Rugs that have been chemically washed to give the appearance of age normally show the same degree of fading throughout the depth of the pile.

Another distinctive feature is the tendency of certain pigments (found only in older rugs) to erode the pile and leave areas of the design with a charred appearance. The culprit is the iron oxide found in some of the natural dyestuffs (oak-apples, etc.) used to produce black, brown and aubergine shades. These pigments are now rarely used, and any rug with this 'corrosive' effect will almost certainly predate the Second World War. This does not in any way devalue these items, and often produces an extremely attractive visual effect. It is most frequently encountered in old Caucasian, nomadic and village rugs, and is much less common in workshop items.

Dates and signatures Sometimes woven into the pile of the rug, usually in the border; these can usually be taken as a clear indication of when and by whom the rug was made. (Copies of old rugs sometimes include the original date and signature, but there is rarely any attempt to pass them off as originals; even if there were, other indicators of age would make such deceit obvious.) The fact that a rug is signed or dated does not imply that it is in any way superior to similar items that have not been inscribed, although it is fair to say that weavers rarely sign inferior examples of their work.

Inscriptions and signatures may be either within a cartouche or in an open form.

1 2 3 4 5 6 7 8 9 0

Stylized Arabic/Persian numerals.

Reading signatures and inscriptions Requires a thorough knowledge of the many different languages and regional variations used in the rug-making countries. However, with the possible exception of a few highly collectable older items, it is only important to translate the signatures and inscriptions on masterworkshop rugs, because the work of different weavers can command considerably different prices. The writing on other categories of contemporary rugs may be of interest, but rarely has any bearing on their quality or value. If there is any doubt about the authenticity of a masterworkshop rug, always consult an independent translator, who can probably be located through a translation service or language school.

Reading dates Far easier, as they are normally written in either European, or more probably Arabic numerals (which are read from right to left), and conform to one of three calendar systems. The most common is the Muslim calendar – which begins on 16 July 622 – and thus most dates found on oriental rugs have to be converted to the Gregorian calendar used in the West.

The main exception involves items made by the Christian Armenians, who occupied much of the Caucasus, eastern Anatolia and parts of Persia, which are dated according to the Gregorian calendar. All dates conforming to this chronology, which are invariably written in European numerals, can be taken at face value. Some very old Caucasian items used the Julian calendar, which was in use in Russia until 1918, but the difference between the two systems is negligible.

Converting the Muslim year to the Gregorian (Western) year This is a relatively simple calculation. First divide the date on the rug by 33 – the Muslim year is approximately 1/33 (or 11 days) shorter than the Gregorian year – and subtract the result from the original date. Add this figure to 622 – the year of Mohammed's flight from Mecca to Medina – and the result is the Gregorian year when the rug was made. If, for example, the date on the rug was 946, the calculation would be as follows:

$$946 \div 33 = 28$$
$$946 - 28 = 918$$
$$918 + 622 = \textbf{1540}$$

Price and value

Price is determined by a number of factors, including the cost of purchase in the country of origin, shipping, washing, import tariffs and the wholesaler's overheads; but by far the most important influence on the price you will pay in shops is the profit margin of the individual retail outlet. Unlike the wholesaler, who normally has reasonably fixed prices, the retailer will charge whatever he thinks the customer is willing to pay. Retail prices are therefore very susceptible to the law of supply and demand. Certain basic costs must be recouped if the retailer is to stay in business; only in the most exceptional circumstances will a rug be sold for less than these. Nevertheless, at any given time there can be wide discrepancies in the prices quoted for almost identical items by retail outlets in the same town, or even the same street.

Local fluctuations in price are usually short-lived, and the result of a recent surfeit or scarcity of sales in a particular market; this may affect either rugs in general or just specific groups. If a particular type or category is especially popular in one country, it will tend to be slightly more expensive there than elsewhere. Import tariffs imposed by each Western country can also vary, depending on the countries involved, and make a small, but not insignificant difference to the price.

Worldwide fluctuations are generally caused by one or more of the rug-producing countries altering their levels of production or the basic cost of their rugs. Such action is normally taken independently, and the effect on prices is therefore limited to items from those countries. However, any change in the basic costs or availability of rugs from one country will have an influence on the market as a whole, because at any given time the rugs from some countries will represent better value than those from other countries.

Price and quality These are normally connected, and – with some notable exceptions – the better the rug, the more expensive it is likely to be. This is particularly true of items from the same group: varying qualities of Mori Bokhara, for example, are normally reflected in their respective prices. This also holds true for items of similar groups within the same country; a top quality Nain will tend to be more expensive than a second-grade Isfahan (and vice versa), while both can be expected to command a higher price than the average Hamadan or Heriz. However, comparisons between items from different countries present a number of difficulties because of the wide variations in popularity, availability and cost of production; a simple Persian village rug, for example, may prove more expensive than a much more finely knotted and better quality item from Pakistan.

What to pay

The amount you pay should primarily be determined by what you can afford. This may seem self-evident, but it is not unknown for people to be carried along by the atmosphere of an auction, or the sales patter of a dealer. The first step is therefore to decide exactly how much you want to spend and then to look at the range of items that can be purchased for this figure or less. This need not be an inhibiting factor, because there will normally be a wide selection of rugs available to suit every pocket and taste.

Most retail outlets, with the possible exception of department stores, operate a reasonably flexible pricing structure and are usually willing to bargain, within certain parameters, to secure a sale. Dealers will almost invariably try to obtain the highest possible price, but the prospective buyer should always endeavour to negotiate. The degree to which this is possible is largely determined by the prevalent market condi-tions, but is also partly influenced by your knowledge of the subject; the more you know about oriental rugs, the better your chances of negotiating a favourable price. You should never be afraid to shop around or take your time considering individual rugs. Nor should you be reluctant to let it be known that you are contemplating buying from another retail outlet, as the fear of losing a sale to a rival may well have a favourable impact on the price. However, the degree of flexibility is limited, and a dealer will rarely sell a rug for less than the lower limit associated with items of similar quality from the same group.

Price categories

The various local and international fluctuations in market forces make it impossible to fix the price of oriental rugs in terms of cash amounts; regardless of their accuracy at the time of writing, they would soon become out of date. However, the prices of rugs from each individual weaving group remain relatively stable in relation to those of others. It is therefore possible to say that a standard Afghan Belouch, for example, will normally be comparable in price to a Yagcibedir, and both will usually be between a third and half the cost of a Russian Bokhara or Beshir. Comparisons between the rugs of certain groups are more difficult because they are produced in such a diverse range of qualities that the gulf between the best and worst pieces may be greater than that between the groups themselves: e.g., the lowest grade of workshop Kerman may cost slightly less than a good quality Russian Shirvan, but the finest workshop Kermans can be over five times the price.

Price is directly related to size, and comparisons should always be made by the m² rather than simply between individual rugs. However, by taking the wholesale price of two common 'low cost' items as a yardstick (Yagcibedir and Afghan Belouch), we can fix the approximate prices of rugs from other groups by referring to them as either plus or minus x per cent. A Daghestan-quality Caucasian rug is roughly the same price, and would therefore be classified as zero per cent (0%); whereas a standard Afghan, which costs between a third and twice as much, will be marked as +35/100%. These percentages are only approximate, because even rugs with identical wholesale prices may vary in respect of retail prices (usually between 10% and 50%), through the appeal of the particular item and the current popularity of the individual group. However, the following break-down into price categories should provide a useful indication of the prices you can reasonably expect to pay.

Where the rugs of a particular group fall into more than one price category, they have been included in the category most closely associated with their rugs; their percentage costs in relation to the yardstick items indicate the range of qualities. These figures are only valid for contemporary rugs, as in the case of older items, rarity and collectability influence the price.

Wealth category Can cost anything over 10 times as much as the yardstick rugs. Apart from very old and antique items, the only contemporary rugs to fall into this category are masterworkshop rugs, and possibly a handful of the very finest items produced by a few 'high category' groups.

High category Between 5 and 10 times more than the yardstick rugs. This category includes good quality Persian workshop items, silk Quooms, Kayserias and some exceptional Persian village and tribal rugs.

Medium category Cost 3 to 5 times more than the yardstick items, and include Persian-style Chinese rugs and some of the better quality items from India and Pakistan. Poorer quality Persian workshop items and most Persian village rugs also fall into this category, as do woollen Herekes and the best quality Russian Caucasian and Turkoman rugs.

Low category Those which cost up to 2 times the yardstick rugs. This category includes most nomadic, Anatolian and Afghan rugs in addition to some Persian village rugs, particularly the poorer quality items from the Hamadan region. (The growing scarcity of Persian village rugs is increasing their price, however, and it is quite possible that even the shoddiest of these will soon fall into the 'medium category'.) Traditionally designed Chinese rugs and average quality Balkan, Indian and Pakistani items also fall into this category.

Approximate price comparisons between groups

Afghan	(+40/100%)
Beshir	(+50/200%)
Bulgarian	(0/+10%)
Chinese (traditional)	(+0/80%)
Dobag	(+10/40%)
Hereke silk	(+1300/1500%)
Heriz	(+20/90%)
Isfahan	(+800/1000%)
Kashmir silk	(+350/400%)
Mori Bokhara	(−50/+50%)
Mori Kashan	(+100/350%)
Tabriz	(+50/1600%)

These figures relate only to the standard range of items and do not include masterworkshop rugs.

Where and when to buy

There are a number of different types of retail outlet in most countries of the West, Far East and Australasia, each of which has its own slightly different set of advantages and disadvantages for the prospective buyer. However, the type of outlet is secondary to the quality and price of the rugs being sold; it is therefore essential to shop around, and not to allow yourself to be rushed into buying. A number of retail outlets will allow you to take a rug home for a few days so that you can see it in the context of your home, and this simple precaution cannot be recommended too strongly.

Specialist shops These have the advantage of allowing you time to consider individual rugs, both in the shop and often on a trial basis in your home; in addition, there is usually a wide and varied selection of rugs from which to choose. The disadvantages are largely those of price. The fact that they carry large stocks and are generally located in prestigious and expensive locations means that overheads are high and these must be passed on to the customer.

Department stores Offer many of the advantages of a specialist shop, often with the added bonus of credit facilities or instalment schemes. The main disadvantage is that the range and quality of items on offer is often limited, and although there are usually good examples of the most popular groups, you are less likely to find a wide selection of village and nomadic rugs. Department stores may also be expensive because they usually buy from specialist retailers who understandably add their own profit margin onto the wholesale costs.

Auctions Auctions offer the most exciting and unpredictable method of buying a rug. Excellent bargains can be obtained, and there is something deeply satisfying about owning a rug for which you have had to compete. However, unless you have some knowledge of the subject, it is just as easy to pay too much as it is to pick up a bargain. It is extremely important to do your homework and to check the prices being asked in shops and stores for a similar cross-section of rugs before making a purchase. It is also a good idea to attend one or two auctions – in order to acquaint yourself with the atmosphere, procedure and prices – prior to entering a serious bid. Do not take too much notice of the reasons put forward for the auction or put much store by claims of 'no reserves on any of the items'. Auction houses have an obligation to the vendor and are unlikely to allow anything to be sold for less than cost. Always check whether there are any payments in addition to the hammer price before the auction begins; it is customary to have local taxes and a buyer's premium added on to the final bid, although these are sometimes included in the hammer price.

The disadvantages are that although most auctions allow a viewing period before the bidding starts, you have only a limited amount of time to examine the rugs, and full payment must be made at the end of the auction. Some auctioneers will exchange items if they prove to be the wrong colour, design or size, but this is entirely at their discretion, and much will depend on the specific instructions they have received from the vendor. If, for example, the rugs in a sale belong to a number of different vendors, it is extremely unlikely that they will be allowed to exchange an item owned by one owner for something owned by another. But if all the items belong to one person or company, as is often the case, then the auctioneer may feel he can reasonably make an exchange without betraying his client's interests.

Private sale Buying from a private individual or dealer can be extremely beneficial, but unless you have a knowledge of the subject, or both know and trust the person involved, such transactions are not without risk. If you are buying from a friend it may be worth obtaining an independent assessment in order to avoid the risk of either side feeling that they may have been unfairly treated. When buying from a dealer, or a person you do not know, it is advisable to take along an independent expert to negotiate on your behalf. Private dealers are neither more nor less scrupulous than dealers who operate from retail outlets, but they may prove more difficult to track down if something goes wrong. A good private dealer can offer the same advantages as a retail outlet, including home trials, often at considerably lower prices. Dealers can also provide a useful service in locating specific types of rug or generally buying on your behalf.

Foreign buying This can be extremely hazardous and it is dangerous to assume that a rug will necessarily be cheaper in the country of origin than it is in the West; rugs on sale in the bazaars in Turkey, for example, are often just as expensive, if not more so, than they are in London or New York. However, the relative cost of living in individual countries, even in the West, can make some difference to the overall retail price, as can any local fluctuations. Most countries allow their citizens to bring home articles without an import licence, providing they cost less than a certain amount, without paying excess duty. The ceiling for exemption from duty varies from country to country, but it is usually fairly low, and you can expect to pay something on most rugs bought abroad. VAT or similar forms of tax can usually be reclaimed at the point of departure (airport, etc.), and even when any excess duty has been taken into account, an item bought in another country may constitute a worthwhile saving. Check carefully with your own Customs and Excise and the other country's embassy before committing yourself to a purchase, as you cannot take the rug back should it prove unsuitable.

Other methods Catalogues and mail order services share the disadvantages of offering a limited selection, and, more importantly, not allowing you the chance to examine the item until it arrives at the door. A photograph is no substitute for the original rug, and items that look superb in reproduction can be extremely disappointing when viewed in the flesh. These may be the most practical methods of purchase for people in remote rural areas, but avoid any mail order

or catalogue offer unless there is a free home trial period or bona fide money-back guarantee.

When to buy Choosing the best time to buy is not always possible, and sometimes the inconvenience of waiting for the right moment can cause more trouble than any financial saving may by worth. Nevertheless, the rug market can be extremely volatile, and a few months either way can make a significant difference to prices. The state of the market can be ascertained by visiting a number of shops and auctions over the period of a few weeks, and carefully noting the prices. It is much easier to keep a reliable record if you concentrate on 3 or 4 rugs from specific groups. Always select popular groups and rugs which represent a reasonable cross-section of the sizes and price ranges on offer (i.e., from a small nomadic rug to a workshop carpet), because prices do not always fluctuate evenly across the board. At any given time, you may find that due to popularity, low category rugs are relatively expensive, while more valuable items are proving harder to sell, or vice versa.

Insurance It is advisable to insure all oriental rugs against theft and damage, however caused. Relatively inexpensive items could be included in a general household policy, but obtain separate cover for more valuable rugs. You should keep a photograph and description of each rug on record, copies of which could be lodged with your bank or solicitor as an extra precaution. Most retail outlets provide a free insurance valuation when you buy a rug. Alternatively, you can obtain one from any accredited insurance valuer. Remember that the insurance valuation is not the amount paid for the rug, but the amount that would probably be required to replace it and, in practice, is rather more than the price originally paid.

Care and repair

Oriental rugs have a justifiable reputation for being extremely durable, but they are not indestructible, and proper care and maintenance will greatly enhance both the beauty and life of your rug. In addition to normal wear and tear, central heating, air

conditioning and a number of household chemicals can have a detrimental effect on the fabric of a rug. But wool is a marvellous rug-making material and, provided that a few simple precautions are taken, your oriental rug will last for many years.

Correct underlay Extremely important. Never place an oriental rug, particularly an expensive one, directly on an uncarpeted floor. The purpose of an underlay (or padding) is to protect the rug from being squeezed between two hard surfaces, because over a period of time this kind of pressure can damage the fibres. There are a number of underlays on the market, but probably the two best general types are those made from solid sponge rubber – which should not be confused with foam rubber or ripple rubber, neither of which is suitable – and those made from a combination of animal hair and jute with a coating of rubber on both sides.

Cleaning Should be undertaken regularly and slowly. Unless your rug is very old or in a poor state of repair – in which case a specialist cleaner should be consulted – the best way to remove grit and dirt is to use a carpet sweeper or vacuum cleaner with beater bars. First vacuum the back of the rug – the beating effect will cause grit to fall out of the pile – before turning it over and going lightly across the face. Vacuum cleaners with extremely violent beaters should be avoided because they may damage the foundation. If in any doubt, it is safer to use a carpet sweeper or brush.

Shampooing Also extremely important because not only will this remove the more entrenched areas of dirt and grit, but it will also put a degree of essential moisture back into the fabric. If the rug becomes too dry, which can happen in centrally-heated or air-conditioned rooms, the fibres of the pile material may become brittle and consequently more prone to damage and wear. On the other hand, if the rug is allowed to remain damp over a protracted period, the colours may run and, more seriously, mildew may form and cause permanent damage to the foundation or pile. Shampooing an expensive, old or delicate item should preferably be undertaken by a specialist company – most reputable dealers and shops offer this service – but avoid the more general carpet-cleaning companies, as the techniques and chemicals used on synthetic wall-to-wall carpets may not be suitable. Shampooing can be undertaken at home using a good quality wool detergent, with

perhaps a cup of vinegar in a dilute solution, which should be applied gently with a sponge or cloth after the rug has been cleaned. The rug should then be carefully and systematically dried, making sure that there are no pockets of dampness in either the foundation or pile, by leaving it out in the sun and then methodically going over the entire area, both back and front, with a hand-held hair dryer. One of the main causes of mildew, a fungus which thrives on cotton, is the dampness caused by ordinary household plants placed directly on the floor.

Removing stains Should be done by carefully dabbing or spongeing with a wool- or silk-compatible cleaning solution for removing each specific substance (wine, grease, coffee, etc.) until as much as possible of the discolouring substance has been removed. The area should then be carefully dried. If the stain proves difficult to remove, consult a specialist cleaner. Never under any circumstances scrub or violently sponge the rug, as this may damage the pile and cause the colours to run.

Additional maintenance measures Protect your rug from damage by moths, excessive sunlight and localized wear and tear. The dangers of insect damage are easily avoided by a combination of regular washing and the use of a compatible mothproofer. Excessive fading can occur if a rug is exposed to long periods of strong sunlight, and is best avoided by either relocating the rug or putting it in storage for the summer. When storing a rug, first have it cleaned, washed and mothproofed. It should then be covered, on both sides, in polythene and carefully rolled against the lay of the nap (the way the pile faces) into a reasonably tight cylindrical form. It can then be stored in a dry environment. The easiest way to avoid localized wear and tear is to occasionally move or turn the rug so that the normal pattern of traffic is taken over different parts of the pile.

Repair Best done by professionals, but some minor repairs can be safely undertaken at home. Fringes or selvedges that become partially detached can be carefully sewn back by hand using a matching coloured thread of the same material. Any damage to the pile or foundation should always be handled by a specialist, however. Similarly, if your rug becomes wrinkled, out of shape or curls at the edges, this should be left to an expert. (Curling at the edges is not necessarily a fault, and can often be a sign that the rug has been very finely and tightly knotted, but unless the curling is rectified, usually by sewing leather strips along the edges, the rug may suffer uneven wear and tear.)

Where and when to sell

Resale value This is impossible to predict with any degree of certainty. Do not be misled by assurances from dealers that all oriental rugs or at least the ones they are selling, will automatically increase in value; this simply is not true. The majority of contemporary items will probably not appreciate in value to any worthwhile degree, at least in real terms. This is particularly true of the 'furnishing' items produced in India, Pakistan and the Balkans. However, some rugs will almost certainly increase in value, and others stand a reasonable chance of at least keeping their value.

Three factors influence resale value: quality, rarity and the vagaries of fashion. This last factor is impossible to predict, and its effects may be rather transient. However, there is undoubtedly a mystique attached to certain groups that transcends the quality of their individual rugs and boosts both their initial price and resale value. This is especially true of Persian rugs.

Rarity is easier to predict. For example, the pressures on nomadic and tribal peoples to adopt a more settled way of life are increasing, and it is probable that a number of these groups may either cease, or radically alter, their rug-making traditions in the forseeable future. The other indicator of resale potential is quality, and, as a general rule, the higher the quality of a rug, the more likely it is to increase in value.

The three main outlets for reselling are auctions, specialist shops, private individuals or dealers. In all cases, before initiating a sale it is wise to obtain an independent valuation, which should also be backed up by your own observations of current prices for similar items. As when buying, always consider a number of offers before finalizing a sale.

Selling to a specialist shop Probably the simplest and most straightforward way to dispose of your rug, although the price offered will be considerably less than its retail value. Carpet shops are normally separated into those which specialize in old and antique items, and those which specialize in contemporary rugs, and it is important to select the appropriate outlet for your particular rug.

Putting your rug up for auction As with buying at auction, this option carries a higher element of chance. You are more likely to have a rug accepted by an auctioneer if you are prepared to put it up without a reserve (a figure agreed between you and the auctioneer below which they will not sell the rug), but this is extremely risky as it could then be sold for far less than it is worth. Even without a reserve, however, your rug may well realize more at auction than in a specialist shop.

Selling privately It is a good idea to obtain offers from specialist outlets, before selling a rug in this way, as it may prove time-consuming to locate a private buyer, and individuals may require independent evidence of the rug's worth.

The weaving category and country of origin of the rugs illustrated are given in Roman type. Alternative possibilities for each design are in *italic*. For a full explanation of the designs, see Chapter IV

1. **YURUK** (p. 134): pole medallion design (nomadic, Anatolia)

2. **AFSHAR** (p. 109): 'animal-skin' design (nomadic, Persia)

3. **QASHGA'I** (p. 123): *hebatlu* medallion design (nomadic, Persia)

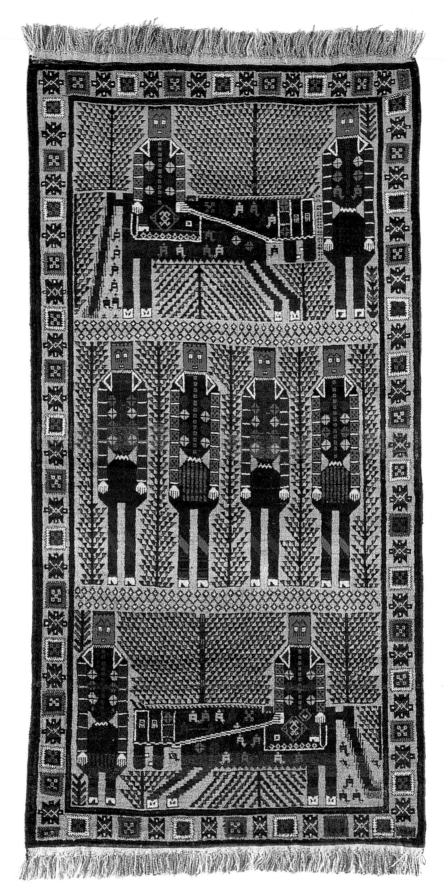

4. **BELOUCH** (p. 111): figurative or 'presentation-rug' design (nomadic, Afghanistan/*Persia*)

5. **TAIMANI (BELOUCH)** (p. 133): 'head-and-shoulders' prayer rug (nomadic, Afghanistan)

6. **MESHED BELOUCH** (p. 111): repeating floral design within multiple geometric borders (nomadic, Persia)

7. **TEKKE BOKHARA** (p. 113): Tekke *gul* design (nomadic, Persia/*Afghanistan*/*USSR*)

8. **BESHIR** (p. 112): repeating leaf design with geometric *boteh* border (nomadic/*village*/*workshop*, USSR/*Afghanistan*)

9. **AFGHAN** (p. 109): mosque design (nomadic/*village*/*workshop*, Afghanistan)

10. **AFGHAN** *enssi* (p. 109): *hatchli* design with a woven *kelim* fringe (nomadic/*village*/*workshop*, Afghanistan)

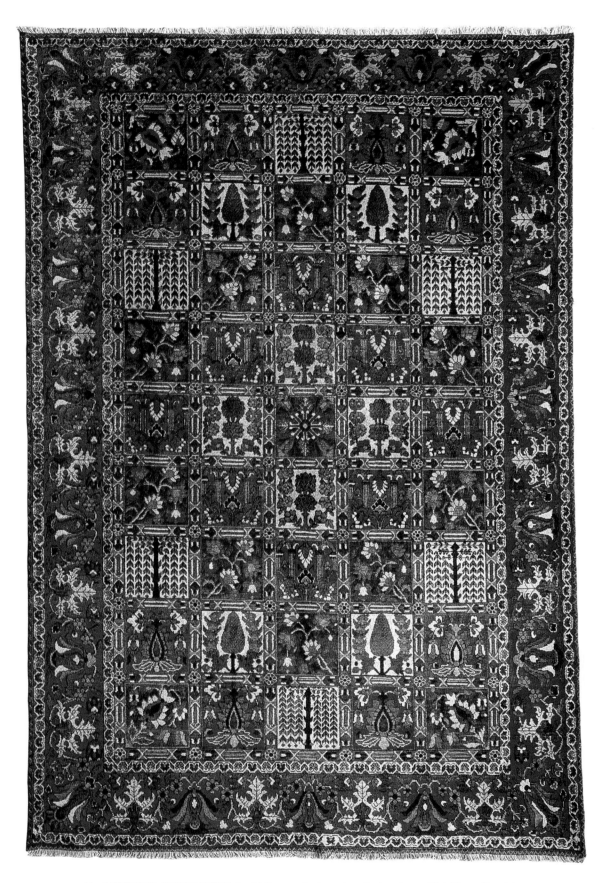

11. **BAKHTIARI (SHAHR KURD)** (p. 110): panelled garden design (*nomadic*/village, Persia)

12. **KOLYAI (KURD)** (p. 130): medallion-and-corner design on an open field (*nomadic*/village, Persia)

13. **BIDJAR** (p. 112): *mina-khani* design with a meander palmette border (village, Persia)

14. **LAMBERAN (ARDEBIL)** (p. 131): triple amulet/medallion design with stylized tree and rosette border (village, Persia)

15. **TUISARKAN (HAMADAN)** (p. 133): pendented medallion-and-corner design (village, Persia)

16. **YAHYALI** (p. 134): pendented amulet/medallion on an open field (village, Anatolia)

17. **YAGCIBEDIR** (p. 125): skeletal medallion design within a double-ended prayer rug, with stylized floral infill motifs (village, Anatolia)

18. **DOSEMEALTI** (p. 114): double-ended prayer rug with triple cruciform motif (village, Anatolia)

19. **KARS** (p. 118): sun-washed rug in Caucasian double amulet/medallion design (village, Anatolia)

20. **DOBAG** (p. 114): sun-washed rug in stylized vegetal tree-of-life design (village, Anatolia)

21. **HERIZ** (p. 116): allover geometric floral design (village, Persia)

22. **FERAHAN** (p. 128): allover *herati* design (*village*/workshop, Persia)

23. **SENNEH** *kelim* (p. 124): hexagonal medallion design on an open field
with *herati* infill decoration (village/*workshop*, Persia)

24. **SHIRVAN (CAUCASIAN)** (p. 133): Perepedil ('ram's horn') design (*village*/workshop, USSR)

25. **ROMANIA** (p. 106): amulet/medallion design with both Persian and Caucasian influences and a cartouche border (workshop, Romania)

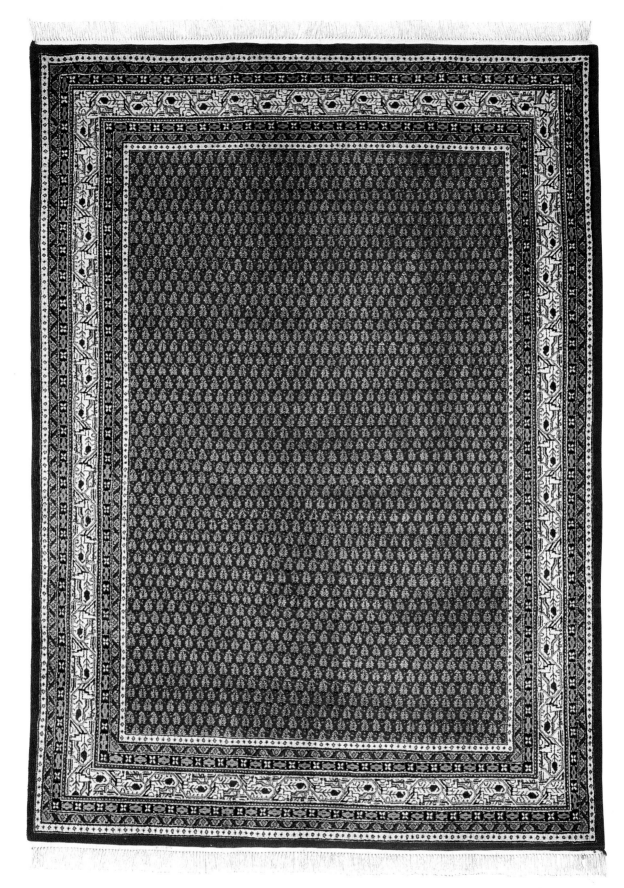

26. **INDO MIR** (p. 116): *mir-i-boteh* design (workshop, India)

27. **MORI BOKHARA** (p. 121): typical repeating decorative *gul* design,
with multiple borders (workshop, Pakistan)

28. **MORI BOKHARA (KAFKAZI)** (p. 121): Caucasian amulet/medallion design (workshop, Pakistan)

29. **CHINESE** (p. 103): dragon medallion design with *Shou* borders (workshop, China)

30. **HEREKE** (p. 115): silk prayer rug in the Kum Kapu design with vase
and tree-of-life elements (workshop/*masterworkshop*, Anatolia)

31. **KASHMIR** (p. 119): vase design within a 'pillars of wisdom' prayer-rug scheme – a paradise rug (workshop, India)

32. **KASHMIR** (p. 119): a copy of the Ardebil carpet (workshop, India)

33. **MORI KASHAN** (p. 122): hunting design with central medallion (workshop, Pakistan)

34. **KASHAN** (p. 118): medallion-and-corner (book-cover) design on a Shah Abbas field
(workshop/*masterworkshop*, Persia)

35. **SAROUK** (p. 124): traditional medallion-and-corner design on a floral garland field (workshop, Persia)

36. **ISFAHAN** (p. 117): Pahlavi-style medallion-and-corner design on a Shah Abbas field – inspired by the Lutf Allah mosque (workshop/*masterworkshop*, Persia)

37. **NAIN** (p. 122): Pahlavi-style medallion-and-corner design on a Shah Abbas field inlaid with silk
(workshop/*masterworkshop*, Persia)

38. **TABRIZ** (p. 125): delicate floral medallion on a Shah Abbas field with a classic palmette border
(*workshop*/masterworkshop, Persia)

39. **TABRIZ** (p. 125): a naturalistic garden design (*workshop*/masterworkshop, Persia)

40. **KERMAN MASHAHR** (p. 120): pictorial rug with famous historical figures. The story
is told in the star cartouche borders (masterworkshop, Persia)

CHAPTER IV

Designs

A basic knowledge of oriental carpet design is essential, not only as an aid to identification, but also as an important means of gaining insight into the rich and infinitely varied religious and cultural heritage of the weavers themselves. Unlike their Western counterparts, who usually strive for individual expression and the creation of a new visual language, oriental textile artists are more content to reproduce the time-honoured designs of their ancestors and seek to express a collective rather than an individual view of their world. This is particularly true of nomadic groups, who have hardly changed their repertoire for generations and who still seek to weave the beliefs and aspirations of their tribe into the very fabric of their rugs, as a testament to their way of life and tribal identity.

The collective expression of an individual nomadic group, village, region or even an entire country is, however, modified by the wider unifying influences of culture, religion and ethnic origin. The result is a fascinating and poignant tapestry in which each rug is both the unique expression of an individual tribe or group and, at the same time, an integral part of the wider forces that have shaped the carpet-making world.

Identifying rugs by their colour and design

It is a common mistake to assume that oriental rugs can be identified by their designs alone. While it is true that certain designs are closely associated, even synonymous, with specific localities or weaving groups, centuries of trade, migration, intermarriage and inspired plagiarism have resulted in a gradual spreading of compositional traditions. This is especially true today, due to the substantial number of high-quality copies coming onto the market from India, Pakistan and the Balkan countries, and it would take an exceptionally brave or foolhardy person to identify a rug without confirming their opinion by carefully checking the weave, materials and dyes.

However, the design can be a useful, if not a definitive, indicator of a rug's origins. Armed with a basic knowledge of the major compositional schemes, the prospective collector or student should be able to recognize many of the more distinctive contemporary rugs and limit the less obvious ones to a few possible sources. This degree of knowledge will not guarantee immunity from mistakes or deceit at the hands of unscrupulous dealers, but it will help to combat the more obvious attempts at misinformation – far more likely than outright deception – and assist in assessing the integrity of any dealer or expert whom one may need to rely on for advice.

Identification, even by experts, is largely a process of elimination based on the knowledge that certain countries and individual weaving groups tend to produce only certain types of design. Therefore, if you are confronted with a rug decorated in an intricate and curvilinear floral-inspired scheme, it is reasonable to assume that it probably originates from a workshop group in one of the limited number of countries which specialize in these designs. Identifying the specific weaving group is, of course, far more difficult, and you would have to gather a considerable amount of information on the individual variations in weave, colour and composition before hazarding a guess.

The first and most important step is to identify the weaving category (p. 11), because this will automatically preclude those countries which do not produce, for example, nomadic or village rugs. Next, by relating the plates and line illustrations to the individual designs, you can use the information contained under each heading in this chapter to limit an item's probable origins (e.g., hunting carpets are usually only made by workshop groups in Persia, India or Pakistan).

After making a general attribution based on design, you should next take into account the colour scheme and tonal qualities of the rug. This is particularly useful in distinguishing an authentic Persian or Turkoman item from a good quality copy made in India or Pakistan. The designs may be almost identical, but, with a few notable exceptions, Indian and Pakistani rugs tend to favour paler, more pastel shades. So if our hunting rug employs pastel rather than rich shades it was most probably not made in Persia, but in India or Pakistan.

More detailed information on the designs and colours favoured by each country and individual group is contained in Chapters V, VI, and VII.

The origins of rug designs

It is impossible to say with any degree of certainty exactly where, when and how the majority of rug designs were first evolved. Some are clearly rooted in religious and mystical symbolism. Others are obviously drawn from a wide range of vegetal, animal and architectural forms; the diverse influences of mythology, folklore, history and the other decorative arts can also be seen. Equally evident is the use of 'heraldic' emblems, or tribal coats-of-arms, and it is not uncommon to find magical and totemistic motifs in a number of tribal and Chinese rugs.

The origin and symbolic meaning of some individual motifs and designs are well documented, but the majority cannot be traced to any undisputed source, and a number of conflicting mythologies have grown up around them. The situation has been further complicated by the constant interchange of religious, cultural and decorative ideas; in common with other artists, the makers of oriental rugs are not averse to adopting a design, or incorporating its most attractive elements into their own compositions, simply because it appeals to their aesthetic tastes.

Figurative and non-figurative
All oriental rug designs can be broadly divided into those which employ naturalistic representations of living forms and those which employ either totally geometric forms, or naturalistic forms that have been so abstracted that their origins are no longer recognizable. As a general rule, Turkoman, Afghan and Anatolian rugs are predominantly non-figurative, whereas those from the other rug-producing countries often use realistic, if sometimes highly abstracted, plant, bird, animal and human forms. Experts most frequently explain this regional division by pointing to conflicting interpretations of the *hadith* (the sayings attributed to the Prophet Mohammed) by the different Islamic sects. The Sunnite Muslims, who are dominant in Anatolia, Afghanistan and among the Turkoman nomads, forbid the depiction of living forms, whereas the Shiite Muslims of Persia – and, of course, the Hindu, Taoist and Buddhist cultures of India and China – are not bound by such doctrinal restraints.

This theory is, however, open to debate. The presence of minority groupings of Shiites in Turkey and Afghanistan, and pockets of Turkish-speaking Sunnites in Persia and the Caucasus (not to mention the ubiquitous Christian Armenians and nomadic tribesmen scattered throughout the region) ensure that there are numerous exceptions to the rule. Equally, political and commercial considerations should not be underestimated, particularly in the major rug-making centres, where the workshops have proved adept at modifying their product to suit the buyer's requirements. Nevertheless, even allowing for these exceptions, the traditional division into figurative and non-figurative regions is largely valid, and you should be extremely suspicious if offered an Afghan or Bokhara rug that contains human or animal forms.

Geometric and curvilinear
A similar, although less consistent, regional division can be made with regard to geometric and curvilinear schemes. This is partly due to the different religious and

cultural traditions, but is also influenced by the fact that it is extremely difficult to produce curved and flowing lines unless the knotting is reasonably fine. It is therefore not surprising to find that most nomadic and village groups produce predominantly geometric schemes, while the more sophisticated workshop groups of the major urban centres tend to show off their skills by weaving sensuous, curvilinear schemes. Although the division between nomadic and urban cultures has diminished in recent years, most of the older, more established weaving groups have retained their traditional allegiance to either geometric or curvilinear designs.

Consequently, the vast majority of contemporary rugs made in Afghanistan and the Soviet Union remain faithful to their tribal heritage and employ predominantly geometric schemes, despite being often of workshop origin. Similarly, the individual groups in Persia and Anatolia have generally retained their traditional repertoires. With a few notable exceptions, curvilinear designs are the preserve of the major workshop groups and geometric schemes are found on village and nomadic rugs. This rule cannot be applied to items from the newer weaving countries (Pakistan and the Balkans, etc.) which produce workshop versions of almost any type of design.

Anatomy of a rug
Medallion (A) Any large central motif used as the focal point of a design.
Field (B) Main area of the rug within the borders.
Spandrels (or corners) (C) Architectural expression used to describe the space between the curve of an arch and its enclosing moulding. In rug-making it refers to the contoured areas at the four right-angles of the field adjacent to the borders, usually only found in rugs employing a central medallion.
Main border (D) The largest, and usually the central border.
Minor borders Smaller, supplementary borders, usually arranged in equal numbers on either side of the main border.
Guard stripes Narrow stripes within the border arrangement. They can be either

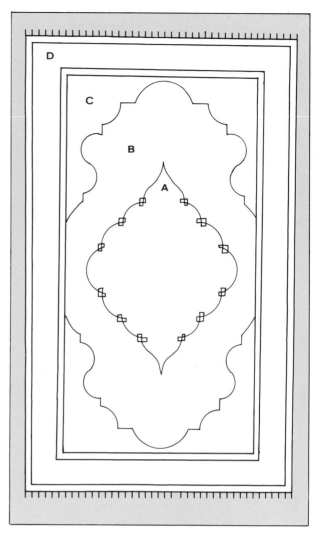

The major design components of an oriental rug

plain or patterned, and are often indistinguishable from the minor borders.
Ground Sometimes used as an alternative expression for the field, but generally applied to the underlying or background colour of any part of the rug (e.g., a blue-ground border).
Motif Any single form or cohesive group of forms (e.g., a bunch of intertwining leaves) which constitutes part of the overall design.
Open field Undecorated or monochrome field, usually only found in compositions with a central medallion (pls. 12, 16, 23).
Variegated field One in which an otherwise uniform allover or repeating design continues over different coloured grounds.

Panelled design The field is divided into panels or compartments (pl. 11).

Repeating design A single motif or group of motifs is repeated across the entire field (pls. 6–8, 11, 22–24, 26, 27).

Endless repeat Another term for a repeating design, which some experts have suggested is symbolic of eternity and the all-pervading presence of Allah.

Dyer's palette The range of colours and tones used in a particular rug or group of rugs (e.g., a pastel or autumnal palette).

Persian and universal designs

It is open to debate whether or not all the designs traditionally ascribed to Persia are in fact Persian in origin, and there is some evidence to suggest that a number may have had earlier links with Anatolia, India or Central Asia. What is not disputed, however, is that their current degree of refinement and decorative panache is primarily the result of the skill and artistry of the 16th- and 17th-century Persian weavers and designers, who took a number of hitherto rather simple motifs and compositions and turned them into some of the most beautiful, elaborate and awe-inspiring examples of textile art the world has ever known.

Floral

The image of a lush and fecund garden is one that is deeply rooted in both the religious and cultural heritage of the Persian people. Not only has the arid nature of the land inspired successive rulers to create the most exquisite and luxuriant ornamental gardens in their palaces and towns; it has also spurred generations of textile artists to compensate for the harshness of their environment by weaving emblems of foliate abundance into their rugs. The weavers were no doubt further inspired by their belief in the Islamic afterlife, which promises that the faithful will dwell in Paradise (also the Persian word for garden). It is therefore not surprising that floral and garden designs feature prominently in Persian rugs.

Allover floral (pls. 13, 21, 38) Designs which feature floral forms without the addition of a medallion, vase or other primary motif. They were popular with some older Caucasian (mainly Karabagh) groups, and may still be encountered on a number of village and workshop items. Perhaps the most popular and satisfying allover floral scheme is the Lilihan design, which forms a substantial part of the repertoire of the Sarouk weavers of west central Persia.

Repeating floral (pls. 6, 8) Designs employing one floral motif which is then systematically repeated across the entire field. Naturalistic versions were found on older Caucasian items, and may still be encountered on some contemporary Persian workshop items. The most common use of this design is in the highly stylized, geometric interpretation found on Beshir and some Belouch rugs.

Garden (pl. 39) Design usually based on the formal gardens of ancient Persia, with their abundance of flora separated by pathways and ornamental ponds. They sometimes take the form of a palace garden seen from above; but more often a garden is simply implied by the juxtaposition of vegetal and foliate forms. Garden designs are most closely associated with the Kerman weavers

Shah Abbas palmettes.

of southern Persia, but may be found in items from a number of workshop groups.

Panelled garden (pl. 11) The field is divided into panels or compartments containing either individual motifs or identifiable segments of the overall scheme. Sometimes 3 or 4 motifs are repeated in alternate panels across the field, and sometimes the same, or totally separate, motifs are used. Sophisticated versions may be found in a number of workshop items, particularly Kerman and Quoom, but perhaps its finest and most definitive expression is encountered in the more primitive rugs of the Bakhtiari tribe.

Aubusson and Savonnerie Designs based on the opulent floral schemes of the 17th- and 18th-century French workshops of the same names. These usually consist of large, naturalistic floral garlands or medallions set against an open or sparsely decorated field. Their influence can be seen in items from a number of weaving groups, but more faithful versions are now usually confined to Chinese rugs.

Shah Abbas

These designs (pls. 32, 34, 36–38) derive their name from Shah Abbas, who was instrumental in stimulating the renaissance of Persian textile art in the 16th and 17th centuries. They consist of a series of slightly different palmettes and floral forms, and are found either in an allover format or in conjunction with a central medallion. They are closely associated with the major workshop groups of central Persia, particularly Isfahan, Kashan, Meshed and Nain, but also feature strongly in items from those countries which specialize in copying Persian designs.

Prayer rugs

Prayer rugs (pls. 5, 30–31) have been used in Muslim countries for centuries, and are an integral part of the religious experience of the Islamic world. An orthodox Muslim is expected to pray 5 times a day on a 'clean spot' facing the holy city of Mecca, and a special rug is an extremely convenient way of ensuring that this directive is obeyed. In addition, the basic design of all prayer rugs reproduces the physical area of the mosque. In early mosques, the focal point for prayer was a sacred stone (the *qibla*), which was set in a wall facing Mecca; it later became customary to enclose this stone within an arch-shaped niche known as a *mihrab*, or prayer niche.

Prayer-rug designs. *From left to right*: the 'head-and-shoulders' format typical of Belouch rugs; the Kum Kapu format of Anatolian and Persian workshop rugs; a Mori Bokhara.

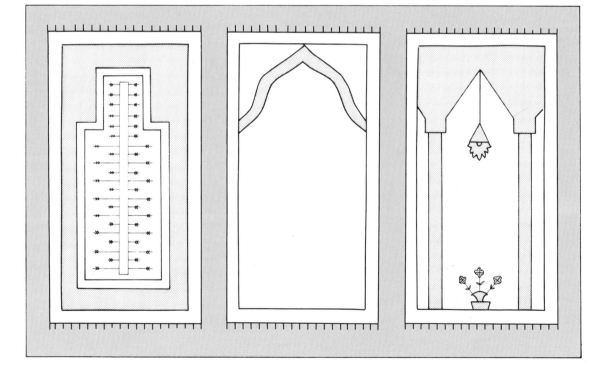

In prayer-rug designs this arch-shaped form is usually found at the top end of the composition, although it is sometimes employed at both ends in what are generally referred to as 'double-ended' prayer rugs (pls. 17 and 18). It represents both the physical *mihrab* of the mosque and the spiritual archway to Paradise, and is often flanked by the 'pillars of wisdom' (pl. 31). The area below the *mihrab*, which is knelt upon when praying, is known as the prayer field, and can be taken as symbolizing the floor of the mosque in front of the *mihrab*. In addition to the prayer niche and prayer field, which are the essence of all prayer rugs, a number of religious objects (particularly incense burners and washing vessels) are often employed. The prayer field is sometimes left open, or undecorated, but vase, tree-of-life and other motifs are frequently incorporated. Such schemes are sometimes referred to as paradise or ceremonial designs (pl. 31).

Prayer-rug designs are traditionally associated with Anatolia and still constitute the underlying format of most Anatolian rugs. Their interpretation, however, ranges from the exceptionally intricate floral-inspired schemes of the Hereke workshops (pl. 30) to the more simplified geometric versions favoured by village groups. Persia produces far fewer prayer rugs, but the design is still found in some workshop pieces. Prayer rugs also form the fundamental basis of most Belouch, and a number of other tribal schemes (pl. 5). India is noted for its high-quality interpretations of traditional Persian and Anatolian compositions; and Pakistan produces some similar items, in addition to those in its more distinctive Mori Bokhara range.

Saph designs Composed of a series of adjacent prayer-rug schemes, and often referred to as 'family' or 'multiple' prayer rugs. Anatolia, particularly Kayseria, produces a number of such rugs, but the majority come from Pakistan and are marketed as Mori Bokhara or Jaldar Saphs.

Vase

This term is applied to a number of compositions employing a vase, or group of vases, as the principal design element. The motif was most probably introduced into Persia from China – where it had been used for centuries as a symbol of peace and tranquillity – and has subsequently been adapted to fulfil both the schematic and symbolic requirements of Islamic weavers. It now forms a substantial part of the repertoire of several Persian, Anatolian and Indian workshop groups, particularly when incorporated as a subsidiary element into prayer-rug, tree-of-life and medallion-and-corner schemes. However, vases are the primary motifs in the two designs outlined below:

Floral vase (pls. 30–31) Variations of allover floral schemes, which use vases as the sources of flowering sprays, and are found primarily on workshop items from Persia, Anatolia, India and Pakistan.

Zel-i-sultan Composed of an allover arrangement of repeating vases and considered by many experts to be one of the most aesthetically accomplished of all Persian designs. Rugs employing this scheme are becoming increasingly rare and, although it may still be found on some workshop items, the only group to use it with any regularity are the Abadeh weavers of south central Persia. India and Pakistan make a few rugs in this design.

Tree-of-life

Tree-of-life designs (pls. 5, 17, 20, 30) are based on one of the oldest and most universal of all religious and mythological symbols, pre-dating both Islam and Christianity. References to a 'tree of life' as the connecting link between the human and heavenly worlds are found in diverse cultures throughout Europe, Asia Minor and the Orient. In Islam, it symbolizes the bridge between Paradise, the world of men and the world below, and still retains a religious significance that is no longer evident in the West. It is usually used in conjunction with a garden, vase or prayer-rug design. Several workshop groups in Persia, Anatolia, India and Pakistan produce extremely intricate and naturalistic interpretations of this scheme, and more stylized, geometric versions are found on a number of village and nomadic items from Persia, Anatolia and Afghanistan. It is also a popular field decoration on Belouch prayer rugs.

Pictorial

The depiction of people and animals is far less common in the East than it is the West, and, despite the fact that vegetal and architectural forms are at the heart of most motifs and designs, the oriental textile artist rarely portrays landscapes or figurative groups. Pictorial designs (pls. 4, 40) based on scenes taken from life, history or mythology, are largely confined to workshop rugs from Persia (in particular, Kerman, Tabriz and Kashan), India and, to a lesser extent, Pakistan. Sometimes they comprise a single identifiable scene or group of figures, and sometimes they take the form of a series of tableaux. They are always distinguishable from other designs which show human and animal forms by the prominence of the figures and the clear narrative quality of the scene.

There is no pictorial tradition in Anatolia, Afghanistan or the Caucasus (although human and animal figures are often used as subsidiary decorative motifs in Caucasian rugs), but some nomadic and tribal groups, especially the Belouch, occasionally produce items with pictorial themes (pl. 4). China has its own pictorial tradition, and copies of Persian schemes are produced in India and Pakistan.

Hunting designs (pl. 33) Feature either human figures (usually on horseback) engaged in a formal hunt, or predatory animals pursuing their prey amidst a fecund undergrowth of foliate forms. These latter scenes are sometimes employed in conjunction with a central medallion, and may possibly be merely developments of the medallion-and-corner design. Formal hunting scenes are firmly rooted in the traditions of the Persian Shahs and princelings who loved to have themselves depicted as noble hunters and horsemen; such scenes represent the nearest examples of portraiture to be found in traditional rug designs. Hunting designs are still produced by Persian workshop groups, particularly Kashan and Tabriz, but are now mainly found on items from India and Pakistan.

Novelty Made by several Persian, Indian and Pakistani workshops, they may feature anything from copies of famous Western paintings to reproductions of dollar bills.

Stylized figures and animals found in Caucasian and Persian tribal rugs.

Medallion

A medallion design can be anything based around a dominant central form, and is arguably the most frequently encountered scheme in rugs from every producing country, with the exception of the Soviet Union and Afghanistan. The number of individual variations is enormous, with each group providing its own distinctive interpretation. Allowing for certain stylistic overlaps, all medallion designs can be divided into two broad categories.

Medallion-and-corner Sometimes referred to as the 'book-cover' or Koran design (pl. 34) because it was evolved during the 15th and 16th centuries from the magnificent tooled leather covers used to bind the Koran; these had themselves been inspired by the inside of a mosque dome, with its central boss and intricately decorated surround. This scheme was first transposed into carpets in the 16th century, and has remained the dominant feature of Persian compositions ever since. In workshop rugs the medallion is usually floral-inspired and articulated in extremely intricate, curvilinear forms (pls. 36, 37), whereas village and nomadic interpretations are generally bolder, more geometric, and not necessarily floral-inspired (pls. 12, 15). Both geometric and curvilinear versions are also produced by weavers in Anatolia, India, Pakistan, China and the Balkans. (*See also* pls. 32, 35).

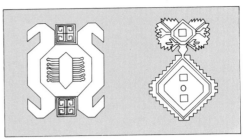

Amulet/medallion Possess an overtly heraldic quality which appears to stem from some ancient tribal emblem or standard rather than the Koran 'book-cover' design. They are distinguished from medallion-and-corner schemes by the totemistic quality of the forms and frequent repetition of the dominant motif (pls. 3, 14, 16, 19, 28). This design is produced predominantly in the Soviet Union (Caucasus), Anatolia and by several nomadic and village groups throughout Persia. When 2 or 3 of these central forms are joined together they are referred to as pole medallions (pls. 1, 2).

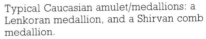

Typical Caucasian amulet/medallions: a Lenkoran medallion, and a Shirvan comb medallion.

Boteh

The *boteh* design (pl. 26) derives its name from the Persian word for 'a cluster of leaves', which it only partially resembles, and is familiar in the West as the primary motif of the Paisley design. Its origins are extremely obscure and there is still considerable debate as to whether it was first used in Persia or India. Equally contentious is its inspirational source, and experts have suggested that it represents a stylized version of such diverse objects as a pine cone, a cypress tree, a leaf, a foetus, a male sperm and the Zoroastrian flame. It is composed of a single almond-shaped form curling at its narrowest point into a loop or tail and is employed as a repeating motif in either allover or medallion-and-corner formats. The size and shape of the individual motifs vary considerably, but as a general rule, they tend to be larger and bolder in village

Variations on the *boteh* motif.

The *herati* design.

The Herat or 'meander' border pattern found mainly in Persian workshop rugs.

and nomadic rugs, and smaller and more delicate in workshop items. The most frequently encountered variation of the *boteh* is known as the *mir* or *mir-i-boteh* design, so named because the village of Mal-e-Mir, in the Serabend district of west central Persia, was renowned for fine quality rugs in this design. It consists of numerous off-set rows of tiny *botehs* arranged to create the illusion of symmetrically fallen leaves.

Rugs employing the *boteh* design were made until recently by several workshop, village and nomadic groups in Persia, but with the exception of a small number of examples from Serabend, Quoom and Kerman, the vast majority are now made in India and usually marketed as Indo Mirs.

Herati

The *herati* design (pls. 22, 23) derives its name from the town of Herat (part of Persia until the last century, but now in Afghanistan), where it is said to have originated. It is composed of a single floral head within a diamond framework flanked by four outwardly curling leaves. It is sometimes referred to as the *mahi* or 'fish-in-the-pond' design (*mahi* being the Persian word for fish), because many traditional sources have cited this as its symbolic origin. In Persian mythology the world was supported by four swimming fish. It is also known as the Ferahan design, as it so dominated the compositions of this Persian town. Although there are numerous interpretations of the basic *herati* form, it is usually employed in either an allover or medallion-and-corner format. In this latter scheme, the field is always *herati*, but the medallion may be either floral or skeletal (pl. 23), which allows

the *herati* patterning to extend through the medallion to create the impression of an allover scheme on a variegated ground.

Herati-design rugs are made by numerous workshop, village and nomadic groups throughout Persia, but are most closely associated with those from Khorassan, Kurdistan, Ferahan, Hamadan and Tabriz. This design is rarely found outside Persia, although India now produces rugs in traditional Persian *herati* schemes.

Other common designs

Mina-khani (pl. 13) Similar to the *herati*, but composed of a single flower within a slightly curvilinear diamond lattice, terminating at its four points in flower heads of equal size, which is repeated across the field. It was traditionally associated with the Veramin and Tehran weavers of north central Persia and can still be found in some Persian village and workshop items. India also makes some rugs in this design.

Joshagan Derives its name from the central Persian village where it evolved over 200 years ago, and is a more delicate and sensuous variation of the *mina-khani* composition. Its classic interpretation is largely confined to Persian workshop and more sophisticated village rugs, but Indian weavers will probably bring their own versions onto the market in the near future.

Harshang Takes its name from the Persian word for crab, but is probably based on either a floral or animal form. It was traditionally associated with Persia and the southern Caucasus, but in recent years it has been incorporated into the repertoire of weaving groups in other rug-making countries.

Turkoman designs

Some motifs and compositions used in Turkoman rugs have already been dealt with in the section on Persian and universal designs. There are, however, two schemes which must be considered separately, as purely Turkoman designs.

Gul

Lozenge-shaped motifs (*guls*) arranged in vertical rows, usually with off-set rows of

minor *guls*, in a repeating allover format are typical in Turkoman rugs. The word means flower in Persian, but is perhaps more likely to have been derived from the ancient Turkish word for family or clan. Certainly, the Turkoman nomads have used the *gul* motif as a tribal emblem, or standard, for centuries. Each tribe had its own distinctive variation, which, if they were defeated in battle or amalgamated into a more powerful

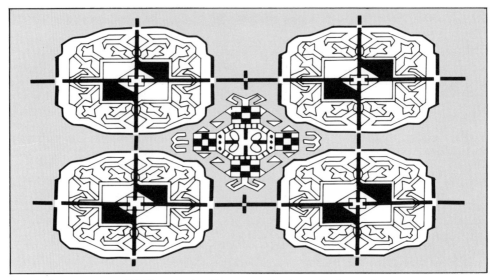

A typical arrangement of Tekke *guls*, in off-set rows of major and minor *guls*.

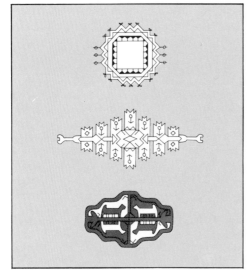

Typical Bokhara *guls*: Salor/Saryk, Yamut Kepse, and Saryk/Ersari *guls*.

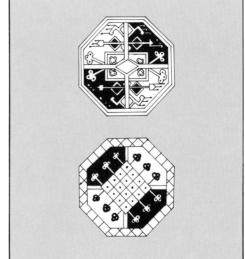

'Elephant's foot' or *Gulli gul*, found in Afghan rugs.

tribe, would often be replaced, or absorbed into their conquerors' repertoire. It is also possible that *guls* possessed some mystical or totemistic significance, but although symbols aimed at warding off the 'evil eye' are still found in some tribal weaving, any deeper meaning attributed to them can now be little more than conjecture.

The influence of the *gul* design is enormous. The Turkoman nomads were no respecters of national frontiers, and their territory and influence spanned much of Central Asia. They are, however, most closely associated with the Russian town of Bokhara, which was traditionally used as a marketing centre for their wares, and today any item employing a *gul* design is generally referred to as a Bokhara rug. The number of these tribesmen has decreased considerably in recent years (due largely to the constant encroachment of urbanized civilization and their forced amalgamation into larger tribal groupings), resulting in a decline in both the number and variety of genuine Turkoman rugs coming onto the market.

However, there are still a number of authentic tribal items being produced, and workshop versions are now made in the Soviet Union, Afghanistan and Pakistan.

Rugs employing *gul* designs can be divided into three broad groups. The first and most important are authentic nomadic items which employ their own tribal *guls*. These are mainly confined to Afghanistan and north-east Persia, although some genuine Russian tribal items may also be found, and are predominantly the work of the Tekke, Yamut, Ersari, Chodor, Saryk and Salor tribes (pl. 7).

The second group are those which are made in workshops but employ authentic (or authentic-looking) tribal *guls*. These items are made in Afghanistan, the Soviet Union and Pakistan, and although they closely resemble nomadic rugs, often employ a range of *guls* (Pendi, Penjdeh, etc.) which do not belong to any tribal group.

Finally, there are those rugs featuring highly decorative *gul*-like forms (bearing only a passing resemblance to authentic tribal motifs) which are almost exclusively confined to the Pakistani Mori Bokhara range (pl. 27). Mori Bokharas may also be referred to by a number of alternative names (including Jaldar, Kafkazi – pl. 28 – and Serapi), and it is not unknown for them to be marketed under the name of the *gul* most prominent in their design. Persian and Russian items are normally referred to as Bokharas, but may equally be marketed under the name of their *gul* or weaving tribe. Afghan rugs employing the typical Afghan 'Elephant's foot' (or *Gulli*) *gul* are rarely referred to as Bokharas, and are usually marketed under the name of the weaving village, district or tribe, or simply as Afghan rugs.

Hatchli (Hadklu)

A design often found on *enssi* rugs, which were traditionally used as door-hangings in the nomad's *yurt* (tent); it is quite common for any rug woven in this design to be referred to as an *enssi*, or a Bokhara with an *enssi* design. There are a number of interpretations of this scheme, but all share certain characteristics. The most fundamental of these is for the field to be divided into quadrants by a central cross, and for each of these segments to be decorated with the same design. Infill decorations may vary, but often feature rows of tiny Y-shaped motifs, resembling double-armed candlesticks; stylized leaf, frond or other vegetal motifs are also common.

The symbolism of the *hatchli* design is a source of considerable debate among carpet scholars. Some authorities argue that it is a variation of the more traditional prayer rug symbolism, and *hatchli* rugs are sometimes referred to as 'husband and wife' prayer rugs. Others believe that it reflects the shape of the *yurt* itself and symbolizes security and the home. Perhaps the most interesting theory states that the physical door-hanging represents the spiritual doorway to the Islamic heaven, which has four gardens at its innermost core.

Hatchli designs are found on Afghan village and workshop rugs, as well as on those woven by nomadic tribes (pl. 10). Soviet workshop Bokharas are sometimes produced in this design, and Pakistan has added the scheme to its Mori Bokhara range. It is much less common on Persian Turkomans.

Chinese designs

Unlike most other rug-making countries, China mainly draws its design repertoire from other artistic disciplines (painting, etc.), as well as from ancient Buddhist and Taoist symbolism, and other religious and cultural sources. Chinese design is also unusual in that its motifs often have very specific meanings which can be literally translated into philosophical sayings, desirable personal qualities or magic charms aimed at promoting health, wealth, happiness or long life. Meaning may be expressed by specific Chinese characters (*Shou*, for example, indicates long life or good luck), or by the particular animal, bird or plant most closely associated with each quality or fate. Sometimes the associated qualities clearly relate to attributes which the animals undoubtedly possess – an elephant is an obvious symbol of strength and

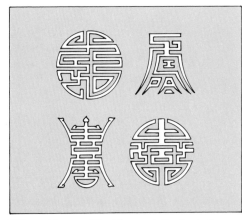

Different forms of the *Shou* and *Fu* characters.

Chinese border designs: 'fret' and 'cloudband' patterns.

power in any culture – but it is by no means obvious why a bat should be associated with happiness or a deer with affluence.

The explanation lies in the fact that the Chinese see a definite social and religious connection between qualities and things. Deer, which were hunted by the rich therefore came to be associated with affluence; and the peony, which was cultivated in the gardens of the nobility, was thus seen to symbolize the rank, wealth and well-being that accompanied this station in life.

Even more peculiarly Chinese are the phonetic associations between qualities and things. Western languages may use puns or play on similar-sounding words, but there are few, if any, direct equivalents to the Chinese tendency to give the same symbolic meaning to an object and a quality whose names sound the same. For example, the

Chinese character for happiness (*Fu*) is pronounced exactly like the character for bat; the characters for 'stag' and 'emolument' (or profit from employment), although totally different in their written form, sound the same when spoken aloud. Whether this unity of symbolic meaning is derived from an accidental similarity in the way the words are pronounced, or whether the common pronunciation came about because of an existing symbolic link, is open to debate. But there is no doubt that this phonetic association is a fundamental and fascinating aspect of Chinese symbolism.

It is impossible in a book of this size to include every Chinese symbol with its accredited meaning, but the most frequently encountered are listed below.

Shou and Fu characters (pl. 29) Usually symbolize long life and good luck. Other characters may also be found, but it is common practice to refer to all symbolic characters as *Shou* (or *Fu*) symbols, regardless of their exact form or meaning.

Swastika pattern One of the most universal of all designs; it is found in the artistic and religious expression of cultures as far apart as America, Europe and India, as well as China, and has been ascribed many meanings; the most popular of these are happiness, the heart of the Buddha and the number 10,000.

Chinese fret Based on interlocking swastikas. It is sometimes referred to as the *wan* design (*wan* being the Chinese character for 10,000) and represents 10,000 happinesses.

Yin/Yang wheel The symbol of creation and life, representing the Yin (female) and Yang (male) aspects of the life-force. It is sometimes enclosed in an octagonal form which contains the 'eight tetragrams' (*pa kua*) representing heaven, wind, earth, fire, water, mountain, thunder and cloud.

Ju-i sceptre Used by the highest deity in heaven, its head is formed into the shape of a cloud. It is often represented in rugs as a cloud with a short tail, and is generally accepted as symbolizing a wish, or the hope that a wish be fulfilled.

Vase (*p'ing*) Symbol of peace.

Table (*an*) Signifies tranquillity.

The eight Taoist symbols These embody the attributes of the eight immortal spirits (*pa*

The eight Taoist symbols.

The eight Buddhist symbols.

hsien), who are perceived in human form through their associated objects. It is, of course, impossible to explore these symbols in any depth, but the following meanings are those most commonly ascribed. They may be found either collectively or individually.

(1) Sword: supernatural power
(2) Staff and gourd: transmutation and the concocting of medicines
(3) Lotus pod: the seat of all power and life
(4) Flute: performing magic
(5) Bamboo: telling fortunes and predicting the future
(6) Fan: reviving the souls of the departed
(7) Castanets: exerting a soothing influence
(8) Basket of flowers: supernatural power through blossoms

The eight Buddhist symbols Relate to spiritual qualities and mysteries that the believer should try to develop and understand. The meanings attributed to each are fairly straightforward in comparison with the subtleties inherent in Taoist symbolism. They may be found together or in isolation.

(1) Canopy: protection
(2) Lotus flower: purity
(3) Umbrella: dignity and esteem
(4) Vase containing heavenly elixir: enduring peace
(5) Conch shell: calling to prayer
(6) Fishes: abundance
(7) Wheel: the majesty of the law
(8) Endless knot: destiny

The eight precious things Taken from the 'one hundred symbols' of the Book of Rites, they may be found together or in isolation.

(1) Pear: purity and perfection
(2) Coin: wealth
(3) Books: the value of learning
(4) Empty rhombus: victory and prosperity
(5) Full rhombus: the wealth in art
(6) Musical stone: blessing
(7) Rhinoceros-horn cups: resistance (to poison)
(8) Artemisia leaf: dignity

The four gentlemanly accomplishments Qualities deemed necessary for a man of nobility and learning. These are usually found together.

(1) Lute: music
(2) Chessboard: chess
(3) Scrolls: painting and drawing
(4) Books: poetry

Animal, bird and plant symbols Arguably the most popular in contemporary carpets, with the possible exception of the *Shou*.

(1) Dragon: power, mercy and authority over the elements. It also symbolized the Emperor. (*See* pl. 29)
(2) Phoenix: the female aspect of the dragon, symbolizing the Empress, which governs peace and happiness.
(3) Fo-dogs (or lion dogs): guardians of Buddha and Buddhist temples.
(4) Unicorn: wisdom. It appears when sages are born.
(5) Stags: well-being and official emolument
(6) Storks, geese and cranes: longevity
(7) Ducks: fidelity
(8) Tortoises: longevity
(9) Bats: happiness and good luck
(10) Butterflies: luck and a happy marriage
(11) Horses: symbolic of the horse that carried Buddhist teaching from India to China, particularly if white
(12) Peony: nobility, wealth, love and affection
(13) Pomegranate: fertility

The four gentlemanly accomplishments.

(14) Peach-blossom: longevity and spring
(15) Lotus: purity and summer, in addition to its more specific Buddhist and Taoist meanings
(16) Chrysanthemum: long life and autumn
(17) Daffodil: good luck and winter

Chinese medallions Unlike those employed in Persian and Anatolian rugs, these may have specific meanings, depending on their inner patterning. For example, a medallion composed from a *Shou* character for longevity does not have the same symbolic intent as one based on the peony, which indicates nobility, wealth and love; the meaning of the inner pattern, rather than the medallion itself should always be read.

A mixture of symbols Used to modify the meaning of one symbol by juxtaposition with another. A common example is 5 bats surrounding the *Shou* character; this represents the 'five happinesses' (well-being, good office, tranquillity, virtue and a peaceful end). Similarly, a vase (peace) on a table (tranquillity), combined with a *ju'i* sceptre (wish) may be translated as 'May you find peace and tranquillity according to your wishes'.

CHAPTER V

Rugs of the major producing countries

PERSIAN RUGS

Weaving region: Iran

Categories produced: masterworkshop, workshop, village and nomadic

For most people, the terms 'Persian rug' and 'oriental rug' are the same. Persia is seen as the spiritual, if not actual, home of rug-making and its name has become synonymous with the finest and most outstanding achievements in oriental textile art. Much of this is due to the magnificent Court carpets of the 16th and 17th centuries which grace Western museums, and the 18th- and 19th-century masterpieces to be found in royal palaces and stately homes throughout the world. Yet these intricate and highly sophisticated masterworks are only a part of a rug-making tradition that encompasses the entire spectrum of the weaver's art.

Persia is exceptional in the number and variety of its weaving groups. No other country can boast the same range of masterworkshop, workshop, village and nomadic rugs, and none even comes close to the diversity of Persian design. It is therefore hardly surprising that Persian composi-tions have not only been reproduced in countless machine-made carpets in the West, but also emulated by most other rug-producing countries in the East. Today most oriental rugs – whether from Pakistan, India or the Balkans – are based on Persian designs, and even China, with its own ancient and unique heritage, is now producing rugs with Persian schemes.

Pahlavi rugs

Special mention must be made of these masterworkshop and workshop items made in a handful of major weaving centres from the 1930s onwards, and generally consid-ered to be among the most technically accomplished rugs ever made (pls. 38–40). When the late Shah's father (Reza Shah Pahlavi) came to power in 1924 he began a programme of sponsorship aimed at elevat-ing the Persian rug industry to levels of excellence that had not been seen since the Golden Age of the 16th and 17th centuries. This patronage was continued by the late Shah (Mohammed Reza Pahlavi) until he was deposed in 1979, and the items produced in the top workshops in Isfahan, Tabriz, Nain, Quoom and to a lesser extent Kashan, Kerman and Meshed are known collectively as Pahlavi rugs. In reality, the term should only be applied to items made under royal commission, but in practice it is used for any rug from these weaving centres produced in the Pahlavi style (pls. 36, 37).

Contemporary weaving In addition to the Pahlavi rugs, Persia produces workshop items in styles that have evolved from those made during the Qajar dynasty (which ended in the 19th century), and there are also numerous village and nomadic groups who, allowing for some minor modifications to the market, still make rugs that have hardly changed for generations. Today Per-sia produces the most diverse and stylisti-cally authentic range of rugs in the world.

'Crab' and 'wine-glass' borders, found on Cau-casian and Persian village and nomadic rugs.

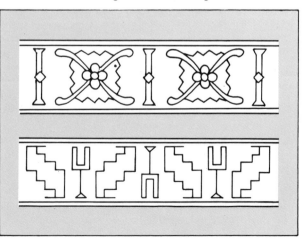

USSR
(THE CAUCASUS)
DAGHESTAN
Derbend
Black Sea
KAZAK
Kuba
SHIRVAN
Kars
KARABAGH
Baku
(ARMENIA)
Yerevan
(Erivan)
Caspian Sea
USSR
TURKMENISTAN
TURKEY
(ANATOLIA)
AZERBAIJAN
Heriz
Tabriz
Ardebil
Yamut
Ashkabad
Merv
(Mary)
Tekke
Salor
Meshed
Bidjar
Tehran
Sanandaj
(Senneh)
Hamadan
Quoom
Sarouk
KHORASSAN
Firdaus
KURDISTAN
Malayer
Kashan
IRAN
(PERSIA)
Arak
IRAQ
Joshagan
Mal-e-Mir
Nain
LURISTAN
Isfahan
Birjand
Abadeh
BALUCHISTAN
Qashgai
Shiraz
Kerman
FARS
KERMAN
Afshar
Red Sea
Iran (Persia), the USSR (the Caucasus and Turkestan) and Afghanistan

Price and resale value Persian rugs have traditionally been considered the most expensive and easily re-saleable of all oriental rugs, and allowing for a few notable exceptions (usually older and more collectable items from different parts of the world), this assumption has generally held true. However, from the mid-1980s this situation has begun to change. Persian rugs still possess an undoubted mystique, and are generally more expensive than those from other countries, but price differentials have been steadily eroding, and they are now generally cheaper in comparison to rugs from other countries than they have been for decades. This is partly due to the relative costs of production and the public's growing recognition that other countries can make good rugs; but perhaps the main reason is simply that the output of workshops has

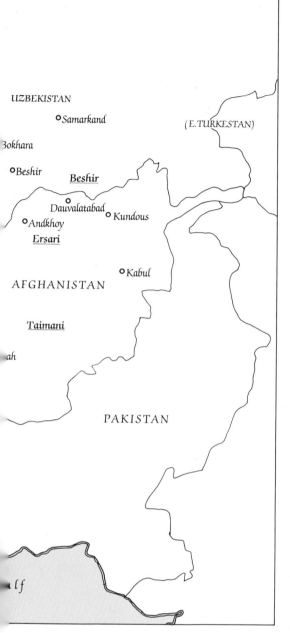

UZBEKISTAN

○*Samarkand*   (*E. TURKESTAN*)

ʒokhara

○*Beshir*   **Beshir**

○
Dauvalatabad○ *Kundous*
○*Andkhoy*
Ersari

○ *Kabul*

AFGHANISTAN

Taimani

ah

PAKISTAN

ı (f

increased dramatically in recent years. There are now approximately 2 million more weavers operating in Persia than there were during the time of the late Shah, and, even if this trend is reversed, existing stocks are large enough to keep the Western markets more than adequately supplied for a decade or so. Consequently, the traditionally high resale values of Persian workshop rugs can no longer be automatically guaranteed, though the finest examples are still likely to retain their value. It is advisable, if you are looking for an investment, to buy the best. In contrast, the production of village and nomadic rugs has generally decreased, and the investment potential of better quality items is probably far more secure now than in the past.

See AFSHAR, ARDEBIL, BELOUCH, BIDJAR, BOKHARA, HAMADAN, HERIZ, ISFAHAN, KASHAN, KERMAN, MALAYER, MESHED, NAIN, QASHGA'I, QUOOM, SAROUK, SENNEH and TABRIZ in Chapter VI, and pls. 2–4, 6, 7, 11–15, 21–23, 34–40.

ANATOLIAN RUGS

Weaving region: Asian part of Turkey, separated from Europe by the Bosphorus

Categories produced: masterworkshop, workshop, village and nomadic

It is common practice in the carpet trade to use the term 'Anatolian' to describe items made in Turkey, although they may also be referred to as Turkish or Turkey rugs. Weaving traditions in this region are extremely old, stretching back to the 2nd and perhaps the 3rd millennium BC. Contemporary techniques and styles can probably be traced to the Seljuks, a nomadic people from Central Asia who conquered the country in the 13th century. The Seljuks' cultural and political dominance was soon overtaken by that of the Ottomans, a more powerful invading force from Central Asia, whose empire reached its peak in the 15th and 16th centuries and whose influence is still in evidence today.

Anatolian rugs were first brought into Europe by Italian merchants during the late Middle Ages, and although they generally lacked the intricacy and sophistication of their Persian counterparts, they nevertheless had a profound effect on Western decorative tastes, and for centuries all oriental rugs were known as Turkey rugs. Thousands were later imported as furnishings for the rapidly expanding middle class, and were simply referred to as Smyrna carpets, because the coastal town of Smyrna (now

Turkey (Anatolia) and the Balkan countries

UKRAINE

ROMANIA

YUGOSLAVIA

Black Sea

BULGARIA

ALBANIA

TURKEY

○ Hereke

TURKEY
(ANATOLIA)

Adriatic Sea

○ Cannakkale
○ Ezineh

○ Bursa

○ Ankara

GREECE

Aegean
Sea

○ Bergama

○ Sindirgi

Kayser

○ Ghiordes

Ionian Sea

○ Izmir

○ Kula

○ Ladik

Yahyal

○ Konia

Nigde ○

○ Isparta

Tashpinar

Yuruk

○ Dosemealti

○ Milas

Mediterranean Sea

Izmir) was the main collection and distribution centre for goods woven in the interior. It is only in the last hundred years that the West has taken a serious interest in exactly where the different Anatolian rugs were made.

The high reputation and influence of Anatolian rugs declined rapidly after the First World War, when the creator of modern Turkey, Kemal Ataturk, set about purging the country of Armenians and Greeks. Approximately 2 million Greeks, whose families had lived in the country for generations, were forcibly repatriated and nearly 6 million Armenians were systematically killed or driven from their homes. These terrible persecutions had a devastating effect on the rug industry, because many of the most skilful and inventive weavers were killed or forced to flee. Needless to say, standards of rug-making went into rapid decline, and, exacerbated by the widespread introduction of poor quality dyes, the reputation of Anatolian rugs soon

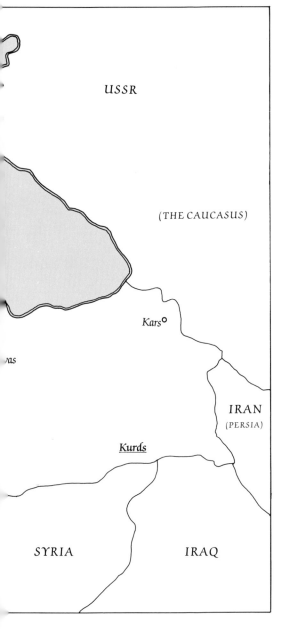

USSR

(THE CAUCASUS)

Kars°

IRAN
(PERSIA)

Kurds

SYRIA   IRAQ

which involved the reintroduction of natural dyes and traditional weaving methods. The result of this innovation was the creation of the Dobag (p. 114), and a number of established groups began to weave Dobag rugs in addition to (and sometimes in place of) their more traditional items. As well as Dobags, Anatolia produces a wide range of village-standard items, which may be either traditional in appearance or designed specifically for the Western market, and some notable workshop items, particularly from Hereke and, to a lesser degree, Kayseria. Apart from the Yuruk, there are no truly nomadic weavers in Anatolia, although a number of groups (Tashpinar, Yahyali and Yagcibedir, etc.) are still essentially tribal and make rugs with a strong nomadic appearance and character.

Price and resale value Anatolian rugs are relatively inexpensive and represent very good value for money. At the top end of the scale, Hereke produces the finest silk rugs in the world, which, although expensive, are considered sound investments. The resale potential of other Anatolian items is less clear, but it seems probable that the finer quality Dobags and the more tribal items, whether village or nomadic, will fare better in the long term than 'furnishing' or 'decorative' rugs. Most contemporary Anatolian items are sufficiently attractive to be well worth buying, whatever their resale value. *See* DOBAG, DOSEMEALTI, HEREKE, KARS, KAYSERIA and YAGCIBEDIR in Chapter VI, and pls. 1, 16–20, 30.

AFGHAN AND TURKOMAN RUGS

Weaving region: Afghanistan, southern USSR and north-east Iran

Categories produced: workshop, village and nomadic

Central Asia is acknowledged by most authorities as the most likely birthplace of the oriental rug, and the Turkoman nomads, who have inhabited the region for millennia, are generally accepted as having inherited the oldest pile-weaving tradition still in existence. Marco Polo's glowing report of the beautiful, densely knotted rugs he

reached an all-time low from which it has only recently recovered.
Contemporary weaving The rugs produced today possess none of the flaws of their predecessors. They are generally very attractive and well made; the dyes are of excellent quality, although there is a tendency by some groups to overwash their items, which weakens the pile (p. 27).

In the late 1970s the government introduced a scheme to improve the quality and profitability of the rug-making industry,

USSR

Pazyryk

MONGOLIA

(EAST TURKESTAN)

SINKIANG

NING-HSIA

Pao Tao

Samarkand

Kashgar

Yarkand

Khotan

KANSU

Ninghsia-Fu

SHENSI

Kundous

AFGHANISTAN

Kabul

Islamabad

Rawalpindi

Lahore

Multan

Amritsar

PUNJAB

PAKISTAN

KASHMIR

Srinagar

CHINA

TIBET

Delhi

Agra

Jaipur

Allahabad

UTTAR PRADESH

Bhadoni

Benares

Khamariah

Mirzapur

NEPAL

BANGLA-
DESH

Karachi

Hyderabad

RAJASTHAN

INDIA

BURMA

VIETNAM

Arabian Sea

Bay of
Bengal

witnessed during his visit to Turkestan in 1280, could equally be applied to some of the finer items being made there today. Certainly, the essential characteristics and overall appearance of Turkoman rugs have hardly changed for centuries. They are almost always red (although a myriad of different shades, from rose to magenta, give them a subtly varied decorative appeal) and their designs are usually based on either repeating *gul* and vegetal motifs, or, more occasionally, *hatchli* schemes.

The Turkomans, who were primarily nomadic and semi-nomadic herdsmen, occupied a vast territory stretching from the Caspian Sea in the west to Tibet in the east, and bounded north and south by the borderlands of Russia and Persia. Today, these ancient tribal lands have been absorbed into the surrounding countries. Turkmenistan and Uzbekistan are now in the Soviet Union; east Turkestan is now part of China, and Baluchistan has been split between Iran and Afghanistan. Despite this, Turkoman rugs

MANCHURIA

IYUAN

Peking
o
in

KOREA

TUNG

Shanghai o

Pacific Ocean

TAIWAN

anton

colours and designs and are generally of good quality. The majority are now made in workshops, but a number of authentic tribal items still find their way onto the market. Russian Turkomans are normally marketed as either Bokharas or Beshirs, depending on their design, and those made in Afghanistan are generally referred to as Afghans or Bokharas, although they may be named after the specific weaving village or tribe (Kundous, Beshir, etc.). Persian Turkomans are entirely tribal and are marketed either as Bokharas or under the name of the specific tribe. The Belouch nomads who roam the borderlands of Persia and Afghanistan are often included in the general Turkoman group, although their rugs are sufficiently different in character and appearance to warrant a separate classification.

Price and resale value Afghan and Turkoman rugs, whether of nomadic, village or workshop origin, are with few exceptions excellent value for money, and in terms of sheer quality constitute some of the very best rugs in their price range on the market today. Although it is dangerous to generalize on the resale value of such a diverse range of items, it is probable that village and nomadic rugs, in particular, will hold their value extremely well.

See AFGHAN, BELOUCH, BESHIR and BOKHARA in Chapter VI, and pls. 4, 5, 7–10.

INDIAN RUGS

Weaving region: northern India, primarily the states of Punjab, Kashmir and Uttar Pradesh

Categories produced: workshop

Pile weaving as it is understood today was probably brought into India during the Mogul conquest in the 16th century (although the native Indian textile tradition is much older) and was profoundly influenced by Persian culture, art and design. Evidence of this can be seen in both Indian painting and architecture of the period, as well as in the rug designs, and Persian aesthetic ideals and compositions remain an integral part of Indian weaving to this day. India was not

have retained much of their original character, and a Bokhara made in the USSR will still possess the same essential qualities as one made in Persia or Afghanistan. However, the weaving of Turkoman rugs has taken a different direction in each country, and there are now certain variations in the overall quality and characteristics of the rugs, as well as in the manner in which they are made.

Contemporary weaving All modern Turkoman rugs are produced in traditional merely a passive recipient of Persian artistic ideas, however. The country had its own rich textile heritage, and it is quite probable that motifs and compositions used in Indian tapestry-, cloth- and fabric-weaving were incorporated into Persian rug designs.

Contemporary weaving India is now one of the largest exporters of oriental rugs to the West. It produces items in almost every conceivable quality, size and design, and has skilfully adapted a wide range of Persian workshop and village compositions to the requirements of Western furnishing tastes. The rug-making industry is based around the towns of Srinagar, Amritsar, Jaipur, Agra, Bhadohi, Mirzapur, Khamariah and Ellora (in order of general quality). With the exception of items made in Srinagar (Kashmir) and Jaipur, Indian rugs are usually marketed under the name of the Persian weaving group whose design has been copied (i.e., as Indo Isfahans, Mirs or Bidjars, etc.), rather than according to their place of origin. Unlike Persian rugs, where the name of the weaving group is an indication, if not a guarantee, of a certain quality, the 'Persian' names used by Indian weavers are totally useless as pointers to the quality of an individual item; they refer only to the design, and must never be taken as indicating that the rug also emulates the quality and structural characteristics of the original.

However, India produces some very good quality rugs, particularly in Kashmir, and the trend over the last few years has been towards finer and finer items. All Indian weavers, whether employed in large manufactories or working at their own family looms, are under contract to one of the major distributors, who tell them what sizes, colours and designs to weave. This lack of individual and cultural expression may detract from their future collectability, but as furnishing items they can be extremely attractive, well made and comparatively inexpensive. Indian wool, although not as good as Persian or Anatolian, is generally better than that found in Pakistan, and in the finer quality items superior Australian and New Zealand wool is often used.

Price and resale value Indian rugs are generally very good value for money, and the better items, particularly silk Srinagars

and Kashmirs, compare very favourably in price with similar items from the more prestigious Persian groups. However, it is unlikely that Indian rugs in general will command a high resale value over the longer term. It is advisable to treat them as good value items which, if they should hold their prices, could provide an unexpected bonus.

See INDO MIR, JAIPUR and KASHMIR in Chapter VI, and pls. 26, 31, 32.

PAKISTANI RUGS

Weaving region: mainly in and around the cities of Karachi, Lahore, Islamabad and Rawalpindi

Categories produced: workshop

Pakistan only came into existence as an independent country shortly after the end of the Second World War and consequently shares much of its cultural and rug-making heritage with India. However, after Partition (1947) the weaving industry in Pakistan took a rather different course. The government provided massive subsidies to the then declining rug-making industry and introduced more modern methods of organization, production and quality control. Muslim weavers who had emigrated from India and Turkoman weavers from the north were brought together to work in large weaving centres in Karachi and Lahore. The industry was revitalized, and since the 1960s rug-making has become an increasingly efficient and well-organized business, operating under strong centralized control. Some Pakistani weavers own their looms and sub-contract work from exporters, while others are directly employed in large manufactories. They all produce rugs to order, with strict criteria laid down to govern the sizes, colours, designs and qualities.

Contemporary weaving Pakistani rugs can be divided into two broad categories: those which employ Turkoman, usually *gul* (Bokhara), schemes and those which copy traditional Persian workshop designs. The former are generally referred to as Mori Bokharas, and the latter usually marketed as

Mori Kashans. Remember that Pakistani rugs use rather thin wefts, which means that their knot-count has to be measured in the manner outlined on p. 27.

Price and resale value At their best, Pakistani rugs are very good value for money, particularly when one considers the fineness of the knotting in the better quality items. But their investment potential is generally rather poor and only the most exceptional items are likely to become collectable in the longer term.

See MORI BOKHARA and MORI KASHAN in Chapter VI, and pls. 27, 28, 33.

CHINESE RUGS

Weaving region: China

Categories produced: workshop

It is impossible to say exactly where and when rug-making in China first began. There is ample literary and pictorial evidence to suggest that rugs were in use from the 12th century onwards, but it is not clear whether these were Chinese in origin or imported from abroad. However, it is generally assumed that rug-weaving was brought into China, probably from Turkestan or Mongolia, some time before the reign of Emperor K'ang Hsi (1661–1722), a noted patron of the arts who may well have encouraged its assimilation into Chinese artistic life. Similarly, it is almost impossible to say exactly where most Chinese rugs were made. Unlike Persia or Anatolia, where each region or village is associated with a specific method of weaving and repertoire of designs, rug-making in China was never based around exclusive localized styles; and although antique rugs may be classified as 'Paotao' or 'Ning-Hsia', for example, this is usually a definition of their quality and style, rather than a statement of where they were made.

Nevertheless, Chinese rugs made in the heart of the country (Suiyuan, Paotao and Kansu) had slightly different characteristics to those woven in East Turkestan, Mongolia and Tibet. The former employed more classically Chinese designs and often limited their palette to blues and cream (Suiyuan

Shou symbol incorporating swastika motifs

rugs are noted for using only different shades of blue to articulate an entire design). In contrast, rugs from East Turkestan, Mongolia and Tibet often possessed a distinctive Turkoman flavour, in addition to elements of local symbolism which combined with their overall 'Chinese' character to create a unique aesthetic style. This was enhanced by their use of brighter colours, particularly warm shades of burnt orange, yellow ochre, peach, pale green and pale raw umber. These stylistic differences have gradually eroded over the years, and today regional divisions have all but disappeared.

Contemporary weaving In terms of price and quality, contemporary Chinese rugs are probably the best value items produced today. The rug-making industry is organized under strict government control and a wide range of items, which conform to exact standards of quality, size, colour and design, are woven in a number of manufactories and workshops in Peking, Tientsin, Sinkiang, Shanghai and other centres throughout the country. The fact that a carpet may be marketed as a Peking or Tientsin is largely irrelevant. It may indicate that the design is based on one traditionally associated with that name, but the dealer may simply be trying to make the rug seem more interesting by calling it something other than just 'Chinese'.

Both wool and silk rugs are produced in a wide range of Chinese, Persian and French

(Aubusson) designs. They are invariably woven with a Persian knot, with a solitary Turkish knot sometimes placed near the selvedge to add strength to the foundation. The materials, whether wool or silk, are second to none, and it is not uncommon for a mixture of wools from different regions – each noted for specific qualities of softness, springiness or durability – to be employed in better quality items to ensure a perfect blend of all the characteristics necessary to produce the best rug-making material. Silk is selected with the same degree of care, and although it can sometimes be a little uneven to the touch, is generally of high quality.

Chinese rugs are graded according to the fineness of their knotting, which is measured in 'lines' (p. 27). In addition, they all fall into two overall categories.

Closed back rugs These top quality items form the bulk of current production. They range in fineness from 70-line to 360-line, depending on the materials and the design, and have piles that can be anything from $\frac{1}{4}''$ ($\frac{1}{2}$ cm) to $\frac{5}{8}''$ ($1\frac{1}{2}$ cm) deep (not including the foundation). The most popular closed back items are usually referred to as 'superfine Pekings' (or just 'Pekings'), although they may also be called Tientsins, Sinkiangs or simply Chinese. They are undoubtedly some of the very best, if not the best quality furnishing items on the market today. The majority are made in the 90-line grade, with a $\frac{5}{8}''$ ($1\frac{1}{2}$ cm) deep pile, but a number of 70-line items, sometimes with slightly lower piles, are also produced. The designs are normally classically Chinese, with spacious central medallions or other traditional motifs predominating (animals, landscapes, floral arrangements) and the colours are invariably pastel in tone (pl. 29). Some rugs in this category employ the French-inspired Aubusson scheme, which is often referred to as the 'aesthetic' style. A number of silk rugs are also made in these designs. They are usually in 120-line grades and have a $\frac{1}{4}''$ ($\frac{1}{2}$ cm) pile. In addition, a number of items are woven in the Peking style, using goat hair; they are slightly crude in appearance, but quite attractive, and inexpensive.

Another range of more finely knotted items are made in Persian designs. Woollen pile rugs of this type may be woven in grades of up to 360-line, usually with a $\frac{1}{4}''$ ($\frac{1}{2}$ cm) pile; pure silk pieces start at 120-line and may be much finer, depending on the requirements of the design. Persian-design Chinese rugs tend to be more expensive than those with classic Chinese and Aubusson designs, as they tend to be more finely knotted.

A third group of closed back items consists of 'antique-finish' rugs. These are based on old Paotao, Suiyuan, Ning-Hsia and Kansu designs; they are woven in the traditional colours, and given the appearance of age by a chemical process known as antique finishing (p. 28). They are usually made in grades of 70- to 80-line, with a $\frac{3}{8}''$ (1 cm) pile, and can be extremely attractive and authentic in appearance.

Open back rugs These are made in 70- and 90-line grades, but employ a different technique, which involves the insertion of heavier wefting between each row of knots, and are less dense and solid in construction than closed back rugs. This poorer quality is reflected in their price, which is normally about 30 per cent less. They can be easily distinguished from closed back rugs by the white threads of inserted wefting running across the back.

Tufting A technique used in some Chinese rugs which involves inserting the pile through a canvas or duck backing with the aid of a 'tufting gun'. The back of the rug is then coated with latex and is normally covered by a piece of cloth. Although these items are technically hand-made, they are not hand-knotted, and should never be sold as genuine hand-knotted oriental rugs. Any item with a latex or cloth back is almost certainly tufted.

Price and resale value In terms of sheer quality, Chinese rugs are probably the best value items on the market today. Only the very finest Persian-style pieces exceed the medium price bracket, and no other country makes rugs of comparable quality for the price. However, their relatively standardized appearance and character, coupled with the quantities available, makes it unlikely that they will become collectable, and they should therefore not be considered for purely investment purposes.

CAUCASIAN RUGS

Weaving region: south-west Soviet Union

Categories produced: workshop
(occasional
nomadic or village)

Caucasian rugs were produced in a region of about 160,000 square miles, stretching from the Black Sea in the west to the Caspian Sea in the east, in what is now the most south-westerly part of the Soviet Union. Until its final assimilation into the Russian empire, this forbidding mountainous region had an almost unbroken 800-year history of ethnic, cultural and religious strife, with a constant procession of conquests and reconquests by Arabs, Persians, Russians, Mongols, Tartars and Turks. The indigenous population, comprising Christian Armenians and Islamic tribesmen of mainly Central Asian, Turkish and Persian origin, were alternately subjected to periods of persecution and forced conversion (or extermination), depending on whether Christian Russia or one of the Islamic countries was in control; this culminated in the widespread slaughter and deportation of the Armenians by the Turks during the First World War. Although the Caucasus was then part of Russia, it was not until the mid-20th century that its borders were defined and political stability was achieved.

This bloody and turbulent history is reflected in the bold, heraldic and violently beautiful colours and designs employed in Caucasian rugs. The influence of Persian, Anatolian and, to a lesser extent, Turkoman designs is clearly discernible, yet there is also something unique and unmistakable about Caucasian rugs, which can partly be explained by the rather unusual development of weaving in the region.

For much of the last millennium, the Caucasus was nominally part of the Persian empire, although its inaccessibility made it largely independent. It was subdivided into several provinces ruled by local khans, who tried to emulate the art, culture and pageantry of the Persian court. They imported Persian carpet designs, and possibly weavers, and young girls were trained to weave Persian-style carpets, working from designs drawn on squared paper. On marrying they would travel to their husband's village and weave from memory simplified versions of the one or two designs they had learned. Some examples of these sophisticated Court items, dating from the 17th century, are in existence today, but by the early 19th century, Caucasian weaving had completed the transition to the 'folk art' tradition that is universally regarded as the epitome of Caucasian village textile art.

Contemporary weaving Caucasian rugs are now mainly woven in state-controlled workshops and manufactories in the Transcaucasian Soviet Republics, and, to a lesser extent, other parts of the Soviet weaving region. They are generally well

Amulet/medallions found in Caucasian and contemporary Anatolian rugs, known as the 'Eagle' (or Adler) Kazak and 'Cloudband' Kazak designs.

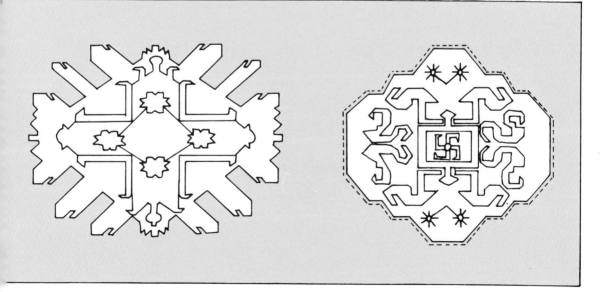

made, using good quality wool, and based on a limited number of the older Caucasian designs. Many of the old weaving districts (Kazak, Shirvan, Kuba, Baku, Karabagh, Gendje, Talish, Moghan, Daghestan and Derbend), villages and towns (Erivan, Chichi, Fachralo, etc.) either no longer exist under their traditional names or are no longer associated with the rugs marketed under their names. A contemporary Shirvan rug, for example (pl. 24), may have been made in the Shirvan area – now part of the Soviet Republic of Azerbaijan – but it could just as easily have come from any of the Soviet weaving centres producing Caucasian-style rugs.

In contemporary Caucasian rugs the name is an indication of quality or design, rather than of the place of origin. This can be a little confusing, because the same name may be used to describe either, and it is sometimes unclear which is being defined. For example, the name Shirvan is given to the best quality modern rugs, but lesser-grade items sometimes employ traditional Shirvan designs, and may also be marketed as Shirvans. Similarly, some Shirvan-grade rugs use designs associated with other traditional groups (Kazak, Daghestan, Erivan, etc.) and may therefore be sold under the name of the design, rather than that of the grade.

The three main grades of contemporary Caucasian rugs, in descending order of quality, are Shirvan, Kazak and Derbend. Shirvan-grade rugs may be further divided into Azerbaijan and Armenian sub-grades (Azerbaijan is slightly finer). Derbend-grade rugs may be separated into Daghestans and Mikrans, although there is little difference in quality between the two. Kazak-grade rugs are rarely, if ever, divided into sub-grades. However, any contemporary rug may be marketed under the name of the traditional group most closely associated with its design. Therefore, judge each item on its individual merits, and not on the quality associated with the rugs of the group whose traditional design has been used.

Price and resale value All contemporary Caucasian rugs fall into the low to low/medium category, depending on individual

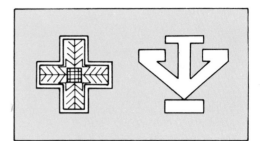

Cross and anchor motifs from Caucasian and some tribal rugs.

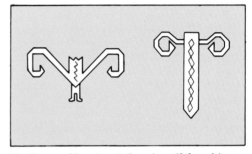

The Perepedil or 'ram's horn' motif, found in Caucasian and north-west Persian rugs.

quality, and generally represent good value for money. Their resale potential is, however, undermined by their standardized production, and, although they will probably hold their value better than most Indian, Chinese, Pakistani or Balkan items, they are unlikely to develop high investment potential over the longer term.

ROMANIAN, BULGARIAN AND ALBANIAN RUGS

Weaving regions: Romania, Bulgaria and Albania

Categories produced: workshop

Rug-making in the Balkans can be traced back to the time when the peninsula was under the control of the Turkish empire. Albania, although not part of the Balkans, is included with Romania and Bulgaria because of the strong similarities in the organization of rug-making in these countries and in the quality and character of their rugs. Weaving in all three states is organized under government supervision, with strict standards of quality, size and appearance firmly laid down. They all produce a growing number of reasonably high calibre, attractive and inexpensive rugs.

Romania, the largest and most influential of the three, makes items in a wide range of qualities, sizes and designs (pl. 25). Each grade is named after a town, river or mountain (which has no connection with where the rug was actually made), but all grades are produced in traditional Persian and Caucasian designs. Romanian rugs may be woven on either cotton or woollen foundations, but with the exception of Moldova rugs (which use mercerized cotton), the pile is invariably wool. The top quality items woven on cotton foundations are marketed as Milcovs, and have 195 knots per in^2; next, in descending order of quality are Olts, with 165 knots per in^2, followed by Mures (130), Brailu (105) and Bucharesti (72). The top quality items on woollen foundations are known as Postavaro, and have 150 knots per in^2; these are followed by Harmon (130), Brasov (105) and Transylvania (80).

Bulgaria and Albania produce a more limited range of qualities and designs, and their items are generally comparable with the top end of the Romanian range.

Price and resale value Romanian, Bulgarian and Albanian rugs represent good value for money. They are well made; the local wool (sometimes used in conjunction with wool from Australia and New Zealand) is of good quality, and they are usually sold in the low price range. However, their resale value is generally poor, and it is advisable to consider them as good value furnishing items, rather than investment pieces.

MINOR RUG-MAKING COUNTRIES

Egypt The most important of the minor rug-making countries. Its weaving tradition can be traced back several millennia, and there are a number of pile carpets dating from the 15th and early 16th centuries still in existence today. These Mamluk carpets, as they are generally known, are essentially geometric in design, but are often intricately decorated with meticulous infill patternings. Geometric designs gradually gave way to more curvilinear, Persian-style schemes during the period of Ottoman rule (early 16th to late 18th centuries) and some of these Ottoman Court carpets are among the finest examples of the period. Rug-making declined after the late 18th century, and only in the last 20 years has Egypt begun to re-establish itself as an important force.

Contemporary Egyptian rugs are produced in and around Cairo, and represent some of the best quality items, in both wool and silk, currently being produced anywhere in the world. They are made in a number of Persian workshop designs, although other styles may also be found. Egyptian rugs are often very expensive – sometimes commanding higher prices than comparable Persian items – but can be well worth the cost because of the high standards to which they are made. They have yet to establish a track record of resale value, and buyers looking for sound investments may prefer to play safe and buy equivalent Persian or Anatolian rugs.

Morocco, Algeria and Tunisia Rugs from these countries have not found their way into the West to any large degree. In addition to the gaudy and often poorly woven bazaar items aimed at the tourist market, there are a number of very attractive nomadic items being made by various, mainly Berber and Bedouin, tribesmen throughout North Africa. They are usually rather brightly coloured (although some, particularly in Morocco, use brown and grey shades of undyed wool), and employ a variety of predominantly geometric designs of Anatolian, Persian and Central Asian influence or origin. These fairly well made, attractive rugs possess an undoubted primitive charm; but as they have yet to establish themselves in the Western market, one can do little more than make an educated guess as to their current prices and investment potential. However, it is reasonable to assume that they will, initially at least, be relatively inexpensive, and, due to the increasing scarcity of genuine nomadic and tribal weaving, may well become more collectable in the future.

Iraq Weaving traditions here are very similar to those of Persia. Some attractive and good quality items are produced, but they are mainly for domestic use, and very few find their way to the West.

Taiwan Exports rugs very similar to Chinese items. While being of quite decent quality, they are inferior to those produced on the mainland and not much cheaper, if at all.

Tibet Some traditional Tibetan rugs are still produced. They are a little too garish for Western tastes, but possess a distinctive ethnic flavour, and the wool is good. (*See* CHINESE RUGS, p. 103).

Nepal Although Nepal has only a minimal rug-weaving trade, an increasing number of good quality items are now being made in the country by Tibetan refugees. They are largely faithful to traditional Tibetan designs, but the vivacious, even garish colours have been considerably subdued to produce pale, pastel shades. They are well made, using excellent quality wool, and are comparable in price to standard 'Chinese-style' Chinese rugs. They are sometimes marketed as Kangris, though a number of other names may be used.

Europe After the initial impact of Anatolian and Persian designs and their consequent fusion with the traditional decorative schemes of each country, European designs tended to reflect the broader artistic and design movements of each successive period. French Aubusson and Savonnerie carpets of the 17th and 18th centuries, for example, followed the Baroque and Rococo elegance of the time with their bright colours and floral opulence, and it was not uncommon for 18th-century carpets to echo the ceiling designs of the rooms for which they were made. Similarly, in England the influence of William Morris and the later Art Nouveau and Art Deco movements can be seen in items of the period. More recently, 20th-century abstract art, with its asymmetrical geometric forms, has been the source of many contemporary Donegal schemes.

Today, very few European countries produce hand-knotted rugs, although many still make flatweaves – some mass-produced and some 'one-off' items aimed at the interior design market. Only Spain and Ireland have contemporary rug-making industries of any note.

Spanish rugs are of good quality and very expensive. Made in a number of sizes, including extremely large carpets, they feature a range of traditional Spanish and modern European designs in addition to more Persian- and Anatolian-inspired schemes. The palette can be quite extensive, but lighter shades of blue, yellow and green are frequently employed.

Very few Spanish rugs come onto the market due to the limited numbers which are produced; they are usually made specifically to contract. Older items have become extremely collectable, and the indications are that the better contemporary rugs may follow suit. Spain also produces some cheap and cheerful nomadic-style rugs, which frequently find their way to Morocco, where they are sold as Moroccan rugs.

Ireland still produces the famous Donegal carpets. They are not particularly finely knotted, but are well made, using thick yarns of excellent quality wool, and are produced in a range of mainly modern designs which frequently reflect 20th-century abstract art. They are often woven to order and can be produced in almost any size. Colour schemes largely reflect the requirements of the client, but both autumnal and pastel shades are common. Donegal carpets are very expensive, but, although they lack the proven track record of Spanish rugs, they may well become collectable in the future.

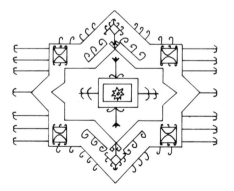

CHAPTER VI

Major weaving groups

The weaving categories referred to in this chapter are defined in Chapter I, p. 11, and the price categories, in Chapter III, p. 36. For explanation of the designs mentioned, see Chapter IV.

AFGHAN (pls. 9, 10)

Country: Afghanistan

Category: nomadic, village and workshop

Price range: low to low/medium; older items may be higher

General details The term 'Afghan' is normally applied to any traditional item made in Afghanistan that has not been classified as belonging to one of the major Turkoman or Belouch groups (Beshir, Bokhara, etc.); these contemporary Afghans, in combination with Beshir and Bokhara, constitute the major sources of the famous 'red carpets' of Central Asia. Originally they were the sole preserve of nomadic groups, but today they are also made in villages and craft centres. Regardless of where they were made, they retain the same designs, colours and general characteristics of the nomadic originals.

Afghan rugs are normally woven on woollen foundations, with between 30 and 160 Persian knots per in^2, using good quality, often lustrous wool which is clipped to form either a low/medium or medium pile. They are traditionally composed in either the 'Elephant's foot' (*see* fig. on p. 90) or *hatchli* design, although a number of variant geometric schemes are now employed. The principal colours are red and blue, with white and yellow ochre as secondary tones; the reds are sometimes subjected to gold washing in order to produce paler, more rosy shades. Some deep yellow ochre (or 'gold') Afghans are also found. Most are simply marketed as Afghans, but they are sometimes given the name of a specific village, region or tribe (Andkhoy, Kundous, Ersari, etc.), particularly those made in Dauvalatabad, in the north-east of the country; these rugs are renowned for their hard-wearing properties and are generally regarded as the best quality – and consequently most expensive – items made in Afghanistan today. Occasionally, pure silk Afghans come onto the market. They usually employ traditional designs, although the colours tend to be more subdued, and are both extremely attractive and good value. Afghans are made in a wide range of sizes, but rarely in excess of 13' × 10' (3.96 × 3.05 m).

Resale value There is no doubt that Afghans represent good value for money, but their investment potential is less assured. The better items, particularly those that can be definitely attributed to an important tribal or village group, are likely to maintain their value over the longer term.

AFSHAR (pl. 2)

Country: Persia (Iran)

Category: nomadic

Price range: low/medium

General details Made by the nomadic and semi-nomadic tribesmen who roam the tableland around the town of Kerman in south-east Persia, and generally considered among the finest examples of nomadic weaving emanating from that region today. The diversity and inventiveness of their designs is legendary, and the finest Afshars possess an unparalleled primitive majesty. The tribe were forcibly moved from their original homelands in the Azerbaijan region of north-east Persia by Shah Tamasp (1524–76) in an attempt to defuse their warlike tendencies, and a distinct Azerbaijan and Caucasian influence is still discernible in their designs. Today, the most common compositions are pole medallions (Diamond Afshars), allover *botehs* (Afshar Dejah), repeating geometric motifs resembling chickens (Afshar Morgi), repeating allover floral motifs (Floral Afshars) and an exceptionally dramatic scheme revolving around a huge central form, covering most of the field, which is believed to represent an animal skin stretched out to dry (pl. 2). The palette consists predominantly of deep reds and blues, but burnt orange and a variety of ochres are also used. Unfortunately, the quality of the wool and manufacture is not always as impressive as the artistry of the design. Afshars can be knotted with between 50 and 250 Turkish knots per in^2 and the wool – which is normally clipped to produce a short/medium pile – may vary from coarse to fairly good. The warp may be either wool or cotton, but the weft is invariably wool. In common with most other nomadic groups, the Afshar make very few large items, and the most frequently encountered examples are of *dozar* and *zaronim* size (p. 29).

Resale value Afshars are exceptionally good buys, and the better, more finely knotted examples can almost be guaranteed to become collectable in the future. As with all oriental rugs, this is less true of poorer quality items, but nevertheless, all Afshars can be considered reasonably good investments.

ARDEBIL (pl. 14)

Country: Persia (Iran)

Category: village

Price range: low/medium to medium

General details Contemporary Ardebil rugs, which are produced in and around the village of Ardebil in the Azerbaijan province of north-west Persia, bear no resemblance to the magnificent 16th- and 17th-century floral carpets, such as the one in the Victoria and Albert Museum, that are associated with this name. They are rather coarsely knotted on cotton warps – with

between 60 and 150 Turkish knots per in^2 – using fairly thick yarns of not particularly lustrous wool, which is normally clipped to form a medium or short/medium pile. Ardebil designs are predominantly geometric, with a distinct Caucasian influence; bright reds, deep blues and ivory, as well as lime and yellow ochres figure strongly in the dyer's palette. The most popular compositions are based around central medallions, pole medallions (usually 2 or 3 connected diamonds) and repeating octagonal forms, but other Caucasian-inspired designs are sometimes employed. Ardebils are very similar in both appearance and construction to rugs made by a number of other groups in the region (e.g., Lamberan, pl. 14) – the name is sometimes used rather more collectively than it should – but items produced in the village can often be distinguished by their use of an ivory field with green or lime-ochre elements in the design. Ardebils are produced in most sizes, and are often boldly attractive and reasonably hardwearing. Copies are now made by Indian weavers, usually with more subdued colours and longer piles.

Resale value Ardebils can be good buys, and although not traditionally noted for their investment potential, the growing scarcity of Persian village and nomadic rugs is likely to ensure their resale value over the longer term.

BAKHTIARI (pl. 11)

Country: Persia (Iran)

Category: nomadic and village

Price range: medium to medium/high

General details Not, in fact, woven by the Bakhtiari nomads (Luri tribesmen, noted for their spectacular summer migration), but by a mixed group of nomads and villagers of Luri, Kurdish, Armenian, Turkoman and other ethnic origins, who now occupy the Chahar Mahal region of south and central Persia. The most popular and justifiably famous Bakhtiari composition is the panelled garden design (pl. 11), but central medallion and tree-of-life schemes are also found. Each individual village or nomadic grouping has its own variation on the traditional schemes, and the quality of the wool, the type of knot used and the fineness of the knotting vary from village to village. All produce reasonably sturdy rugs, however, with a knot-count of between 60 and 200 per in². The small village of Chahal Shotur produces what are generally considered the finest examples of Bakhtiari weaving; and the major town in the region, Shahr Kurd, whose items can be distinguished by their use of the Persian knot (most other villages use the Turkish knot), is noted for medallion rugs reminiscent of pre-Pahlavi Isfahans. The Bakhtiari palette is usually dominated by deep reds, bright blues, yellow ochre, bottle green, orange ochres and browns. Normally, all rugs are marketed as Bakhtiaris, but sometimes they may be named after the specific village – Feridan, Farah Dumbah, Boldaji, Saman, Bain, etc. – and occasionally the more finely knotted items are referred to as Bibibaffs, which literally means 'woman's knot'. Bakhtiaris are generally made in *dozar* and *kellegi* sizes, and also in the rather unusual dimensions, for village and nomadic items, of c. $10' \times 6\frac{1}{2}'$ (3.05 × 1.98 m) and $12' \times 9'$ (3.66 × 2.74 m).

Resale value Bakhtiaris can be exceptionally attractive, and are amongst the most collectable examples of contemporary Persian tribal weaving. Consequently, their investment potential is sound.

BELOUCH (pls. 4, 5, 6)

Country: Persia (Iran) and Afghanistan

Category: nomadic

Price range: low to low/medium

General details Inexpensive, well made rugs, produced in a wide variety of designs, that consistently combine tribal authenticity with a delightful, if somewhat primitive, decorative charm. The Belouch (or Baluchi) are a large tribal grouping who roam the vast border region between eastern Persia and western Afghanistan – and not, as the name would imply, the province of Baluchistan in south-east Persia – although some tribes have been known to drift into

Pakistan. The vast majority of Belouch rugs are made by the nomadic tribesmen, but a small number are woven in the villages around Firdaus in central Khorassan, by people of Arab extraction. However, all Belouchs are produced in the same way and can justifiably be referred to as nomadic rugs. They are normally woven on woollen foundations (although cotton has been used in recent years) with between 60 and 100 Persian knots per in²; the pile wool, although not particularly lustrous, is generally of excellent quality. Belouch designs are usually confined to prayer rugs (pl. 5 and fig. on p. 85) and repeating allover geometrical motifs, although some figurative compositions, often referred to as 'figurative' or 'presentation' rugs, are sometimes produced (pl. 4). Within this limited repertoire, a wide variety of motifs and decorative schemes may be found. In prayer rugs, the most common field decorations are highly stylized tree-of-life, leaf, vegetal and geometric schemes, but architectural (pl. 9), *boteh* and *gul*-like patterns are also employed. In repeating allover compositions the motifs may be either vegetal-inspired or entirely geometric, but they are nearly always highly abstracted. These allover compositions are similar to those of the Beshir, but a Belouch can usually be recognized by a tendency to enclose motifs within a lattice, and by the use of strong white or yellow ochre outlines, particularly in the border. The Belouch palette is dominated by shades of red and blue; camel and beige are also employed, either as pigments or by using natural, undyed wool.

There are a number of sub-tribes and villages within the collective Belouch group whose items may be marketed under their individual names – these include the Mushwani, Nishapur, Dokhtar-e-Ghazi, Koudani and Haft Bolah nomads and the village of Chichaksu – but most Belouch rugs are sold as either Meshed or Herat Belouch. The former are made in Persia (Meshed being the principal city in the region) and are characterized by their stiffer 'feel', more sombre colouring and use of allover repeating designs (pl. 6). Herat Belouch are made in Afghanistan (the city of Herat being a major collection point) and are generally softer, floppier and more brightly coloured than those made in Persia; they normally employ prayer-rug designs. There is little to choose in quality between the best items from each country, but Meshed Belouch are rarer and may consequently be slightly more expensive. In common with most nomadic items, Belouch rugs are made in relatively small sizes – c. 5′ × 3′ (1.52 × 0.91 m) up to 7′ × 4′ (2.13 × 1.22 m) being the norm – but runners and carpets are sometimes produced. Carpets, because of their rarity, may be proportionally more expensive than rugs.

Resale value A good Belouch is arguably the best buy amongst all contemporary nomadic rugs. They have been some of the most eminently collectable items for decades and there is no reason why this should change. You are unlikely to make large profits investing in a Belouch, but a good quality item should do more than hold its own against inflation, and rugs from some of the sub-tribes are becoming increasingly rare.

BESHIR (pl. 8)

Country: Afghanistan and the Soviet Union

Category: nomadic, village and workshop

Price range: low/medium to medium

General details Extremely attractive and sturdy rugs originally made by Turkoman nomads who roamed the border regions of Turkmenistan, Uzbekistan and Afghanistan. The name was probably derived from a small town to the south of Bokhara, in the west of Turkmenistan (now incorporated into the Soviet Union), which is believed to have been the major marketing centre for their rugs. Today, Beshir rugs are produced by nomads and villagers in Afghanistan and in state-controlled workshops in the Soviet Union. Both nomadic and workshop Beshirs retain their essentially tribal characteristics; in fact, Russian Beshirs are generally considered the finest and most traditionally authentic items currently produced in the Soviet Union, and Afghan Beshirs are among the very best contemporary tribal rugs. All Beshirs are quite finely knotted for essen-

tially nomadic items, with between 60 and 160 Persian knots per in^2, and the pile wool (normally clipped low/medium to medium) is generally of good quality. Woollen foundations are common in both countries, although some Afghan tribesmen use a mixture of wool and goat's hair. A range of traditional designs are employed. Unlike the majority of Turkoman nomads, the Beshir do not use *guls* as their dominant motif; instead they employ a variety of highly stylized leaf, frond and other vegetal (and occasionally animal) forms in allover repeating patterns (pl. 8). The palette is also somewhat innovative; although dominated by the typically Turkoman deep reds and blues, it is often enlivened by paler, more joyous shades. This vital yet dignified combination of colour and form makes Beshirs among the most aesthetically satisfying of all Turkoman rugs. They are normally made in large rug and small carpet sizes, usually rather longer than they are wide, and in runners of various dimensions. Indian weavers also produce a few items in Beshir designs.

Resale value Beshirs are generally good buys, both because of their quality and appearance, and the nomadic items in particular should make sound investments. Old Beshirs are very collectable and expensive.

BIDJAR (pl. 13)

Country: Persia (Iran)

Category: village

Price range: medium to high

General details Superb rugs woven in a small village about 30 miles from the town of Senneh in Kurdistan, and often referred to as the 'iron rugs of Persia' because of their strength and durability. The knotting on Bidjar rugs is not especially fine, with between 100 and 220 Turkish knots per in^2, but the Bidjar weavers use a special tool, not unlike a huge claw, to beat the weft strands together until they form an exceptionally compact foundation for the pile. This makes the rug extremely dense and heavy, and one should never fold a Bidjar because the warp and weft are so tightly pressed together that they could easily break; it also makes them among the most hard-wearing items produced anywhere in the world. Bidjars are usually woven on cotton warps, although wool is not unknown. For the pile good quality lustrous wool is used and may be clipped low/medium to medium/high. A number of designs are employed, but floral, *herati* and *mina-khani* schemes, with or without a central medallion, are those most frequently encountered (pl. 13). The palette is essentially rich and penumbral, with dark blues, cherry red and bottle green providing the most common ground colours, and ivory, ochres and turquoise dominating the motifs; the finest items are as aesthetically satisfying as they are structurally sound. Bidjar designs, particularly floral medallion and *herati* schemes, are copied by Indian weavers, but are easily distinguished from the originals by their paler, more pastel colours; Indo-Bidjars possess none of the structural qualities of Persian Bidjars. Both Indian and Persian items are produced in all standard Persian sizes, from small mats to carpets.

Resale value Bidjars represent excellent value and are one of the safer investments. Not only are they extremely durable, but due to the very small numbers produced each year, they are also becoming increasingly rare.

BOKHARA (pl. 7)

Country: Afghanistan, Persia (Iran) and the Soviet Union

Category: nomadic, village and workshop

Price range: low/medium to medium

General details Bokhara is a major city in Turkmenistan (formerly Turkestan, but now part of the Soviet Union), which occupied a strategic position on the ancient silk route to the East. It acted as an important marketing and religious centre – the name is derived from the Sanskrit word for monastery – and a number of Turkoman tribes, mainly the Tekke, traditionally used it as a centre for purchasing provisions and selling their rugs. Originally, the term 'Bokhara' was applied to any rug marketed in the town, but today it refers only to those items which employ the traditional tribal *gul* motifs in their design. Contemporary Bokharas are made by a number of nomadic and seminomadic weavers in Afghanistan and northeast Persia (and, more recently, by Afghan migrants in the border country of west Pakistan) who belong to the Tekke, Yamut, Saryk, Ersari and other Turkoman tribes. In the Soviet Union, the majority of Bokharas are woven in state-controlled workshops in Merv (Mary), Ashkabad and numerous small villages stretching all the way to the Caspian Sea. They use both the *guls* of existing tribes (Tekke, etc.) and modern variations which, despite authentic-sounding names (e.g., Penjdeh) do not relate to a specific tribe. Afghanistan also produces items with both authentic and modern *guls*, but the *guls* in Persian Bokharas are usually confined to those of the Tekke (pl. 7) and Yamut tribes (*see* fig. on p. 90).

There are some broad differences between the rugs produced in each country, as well as by individual tribes, but there are no overall disparities in quality, and all Bokharas are justifiably regarded as among the finer examples of tribal textile art. They are normally woven on woollen warps, with between 160 and 320 Persian knots per in^2, and the pile wool, which is generally clipped low, is extremely silky and very hard-wearing. The palette is generally limited to deep reds and blues, with ivory and yellow ochre highlights, but the variation in tones, ranging from rose to deepest madder, adds significantly to the variety of their visual appeal. Bokharas are usually fairly small – from *c.* 5′ × 3′ (1.52 × 0.91 m) to *dozar* size – but runners and some carpet sizes are occasionally made.

Pakistani weavers have successfully adapted the *gul* design to Western demands (pl. 27), but these items belong to an entirely different category of rug (see MORI BOKHARA, p. 121).

Resale value Bokharas have been collected consistently over the years and there is no reason why their popularity should change; they can therefore be considered sound investments, particularly those which have a distinct tribal origin.

DOBAG (pl. 20)

Country: Anatolia (Turkey)

Category: village

Price range: low to low/medium

General details Dobags are not made by any specific weaving group: the name is an acronym for a project sponsored by the Turkish government, which sought to re-establish the traditional methods and materials of Anatolian weaving and ensure that all items conformed to strict criteria. The most important aims were to re-introduce natural dyes, to regularize the fineness of the knotting into specific grades and to control the quality of the wool. Unfortunately, these grades are often ignored by retail outlets, and potential customers have to assess the varying qualities for themselves.

However, all Dobags use natural dyes wherever possible, and are generally attractive and well made. They employ a wide variety of traditional Anatolian, and to a lesser extent Caucasian-inspired designs, and their colour schemes range from rich, almost primary shades to delicate pastel, depending on the washing process. Because Dobags are not made by any one identifiable village group (a number of villages participate in this scheme) they may be marketed under a variety of names (Dobag or Avajack, etc.) or simply referred to as Turkish or Anatolian rugs. If the name of a particular item is unfamiliar ask the dealer whether it is a Dobag, or simply a rug belonging to one of the less well-known weaving groups. It is also important to find out the particular quality or grade, as these are not usually implied in the name.

Dobags are made in a number of sizes, but *ceyrek* and *seccade* are the most common; as with most village items, carpet sizes are rare.

Resale value Dobags are a relatively recent innovation, and it is therefore impossible to predict their investment potential with any certainty. However, they are generally attractive and durable, and have the added visual appeal of natural dyes; provided over-production is avoided, they should retain their value reasonably well.

DOSEMEALTI (pl. 18)

Country: Anatolia (Turkey)

Category: village

Price range: low to low/medium

General details Exceptionally attractive rugs woven in and around the village of Dosemealti. They are not especially finely knotted, with *c.* 70 to 120 Turkish knots per in^2, but the knotting is regular, and thick yarns of good quality wool, normally cropped to form a medium pile, are used in conjunction with the traditional woollen foundation. Dosemealti designs are closely related to those of the Luri nomads and focus on two broad compositional schemes: the first is based on a central row of three cruciform motifs (pl. 18), and the second features large repeating frond forms, which resemble vegetal candlesticks; both schemes are normally contained within an elongated hexagonal double-ended prayer-rug format. Reds, blues and a warm bottle green, with hints of ochre, are the dominant colours; these can be either rich or muted, depending on the type of wash, but they are usually well balanced and harmonious. Dosemealti rugs are made in a number of sizes, but *seccade* is the most common. Dosemealti weavers also produce items in Caucasian designs which tend to be slightly more expensive than their traditional rugs.

Resale value Excellent value; although they are not considered to have a high investment potential, they should keep their value to an acceptable degree.

HAMADAN (pl. 15)

Country: Persia (Iran)

Category: village

Price range: low to medium/high

General details Made in dozens of small villages in a wide radius around the west central Persian city of Hamadan, they constitute some of the shoddiest and most unattractive items made anywhere in Persia today. However, there are also some well made and visually exciting examples produced in the region, and even the poorer examples possess a certain primitive charm and village authenticity which is often the focal point of collectable appeal. Each village or small group of villages has its own distinct variations, but there are a few overall characteristics that unify them into one relatively cohesive group. The Hamadan palette is dominated by reds, blues and whites, with greens, gold and yellow ochres as subsidiary hues; the design repertoire is based on geometric medallion-and-corner, *herati* and *boteh* schemes, and those which employ detached floral sprays in an allover arrangement, similar to those employed in the nearby village of Sarouk.

The Sarouk scheme is mainly produced in the villages of Dergezine, Kabutrahang, Mehriban, Kasvin and Injelas, and by the Mongol Borchalu tribesmen, who occupy a small group of villages in a remote valley east of Hamadan and north-west of Sarouk. With the possible exception of Kasvin, and to a lesser degree Kabutrahang, these villages also produce items in *herati*, *boteh* and sometimes medallion-and-corner schemes. In terms of quality, Injelas, Borchalu and Kasvin (although this village now produces very little) are generally regarded as the best, and their finest items can be excellent. Reasonable quality medallion schemes are made in the village of Tuisarkan (pl. 15). The village of Khamseh (not to be confused with the nomadic federation of the same name, who live in the Fars province of southern Persia) produces basic but quite attractive medallion and *herati* schemes, and the unmistakable Mazlaghan rugs, with their famous zig-zag or 'lightning' design are made in the villages of Mazlaghan, Norberan and Kerdar (*see* fig. on p. 28). Another distinctive rug woven in the region, which usually features a *herati* scheme either with or without a central medallion, is known as a Bibicabad and is one of the least attractive Hamadan items. The poorest quality rugs from the region are often referred to as Mosuls.

All Hamadan rugs are woven on cotton foundations, with 30 to 100 Turkish knots per in^2, using good quality pile wool, sometimes mixed with camel hair, which is clipped medium to medium/long. They are made in a wide range of sizes, though very large items are rare.

A number of Hamadan designs are now copied by Indian weavers in qualities that often compare favourably with the originals, if lacking their aesthetic panache. (The Hamadan village of Mehriban should not be confused with the village of the same name in the Heriz region.) Additional information on the more important Hamadan villages is contained in Chapter VII.

Resale value The overall investment potential of Hamadans has tended to be rather low, but the finer examples – in particular older Injelas and some Borchalus – have always been collectable. The growing commercialization of rug-making in Persia may result in the more distinctive and authentic village products increasing in value over the longer term.

HEREKE (pl. 30)

Country: Anatolia (Turkey)

Category: workshop and masterworkshop

Price range: medium to wealth

General details The town of Hereke in northwest Anatolia produces the finest silk rugs made anywhere in the world today. The skill, artistry and technical virtuosity of the Hereke weavers is second to none, and the items they produce are justifiably regarded as among the most distinguished and valuable examples of contemporary textile art. Their silk rugs are normally woven on silk foundations, although cotton may sometimes be used, with an average of 700 to 800 Turkish knots per in^2; it is not uncommon for gilded metallic threads to be woven into the pile. The compositional repertoire encompasses a wide range of traditional Anatolian and Persian schemes, mainly of floral origin, but it is perhaps most closely associated with classic Ottoman prayer-rug designs, which are normally articulated in intricate detail and often contain inscribed cartouches in the borders (pl. 30). Various shades of red, blue, yellow and gold ochres and bottle green dominate the palette, and the implicit richness of their tones is enhanced by the iridescence of the fine quality silk. However, as with all oriental rugs, some items are better than others, and one should always examine each rug carefully in order to assess the fineness of the knotting and the symmetry and articulation of the design. The most important contemporary masterweaver in Hereke is Ozapek, who is regarded as the most accomplished contemporary Anatolian textile artist; his finest works belong to the masterworkshop class.

Hereke weavers also produce good quality woollen items, normally woven on cotton foundations, with between 240 and 420 Turkish knots per in^2; the pile, which is normally clipped low to medium, is of good quality wool. A wide range of traditional – mainly floral-inspired – Anatolian and Persian designs are employed, but the colours are generally slightly more pastel than those used in silk items. Woollen Herekes are made in a range of sizes, including large carpets, but silk items are usually confined to 5′ × 3′ (1.52 × 0.91 m) and 6′ × 4′ (1.83 × 1.22 m).

Resale value The finest silk Herekes, particularly Ozapeks, make sound investments, but the resale potential of lower quality items is less secure. Good quality woollen items may also stand a chance of maintaining their value.

HERIZ (pl. 21)

Country: Persia (Iran)

Category: village

Price range: low to medium/high

General details Made in the town of Heriz in north-west Persia and in a number of outlying villages stretching to Tabriz. Despite this proximity to Tabriz, Heriz rugs possess an appearance and character that is unmistakably their own. The dominant composition is based on a huge angular central medallion, set against a field of geometrically sylized floral forms, within a framework of echoing, and inwardly decorated corners. This boldly heraldic scheme is usually coloured in either strong or slightly muted shades of brick red, burnt orange and occasionally deep blues, with ivory, yellow ochre and paler reds and blues

providing the secondary hues. At its best, it is one of the most powerful Persian decorative schemes.

This design is most closely associated with the town itself, which also produces equally heraldic allover floral schemes (pl. 21), with a number of slight variations being produced in the surrounding villages. The most frequently encountered of these are from Mehriban, which often employs the same floral decorations in an allover format, and Ahar, a village noted for its well made, tightly woven rugs in slightly curvilinear medallion-and-corner designs. The knotcount of Heriz rugs is not particularly high, but they are compact and durable, with good quality wool normally clipped low/medium to medium, and are generally regarded as the best of the more coarsely woven Persian rugs. The finest examples are made in Heriz and Ahar; slightly inferior, though very reasonable items are produced in Mehriban. The quality of Goeravan rugs is comparatively low.

Heriz rugs are produced in a number of sizes, including carpets, but small rugs are rare. Indian weavers now make copies of Heriz designs (sometimes employing the typical Heriz medallion on an open field), but with a few notable exceptions, they are rather crude imitations of the originals. (Mehriban, in the Heriz region, should not be confused with the village of the same name in the Hamadan district.)

Resale value Because of their durability and reasonable price, the better quality Heriz rugs – particularly those made in the town itself and, to a lesser degree, those from Ahar – are fair investments. The growing scarcity of authentic Persian village and tribal items may lead to all Heriz rugs becoming more collectable in the future.

INDO MIR (pl. 26)

Country: India

Category: workshop

Price range: low to low/medium

General details Indian versions of the *mir-i-boteh* design are produced in numerous workshops throughout the country – but mainly in the Bhadohi-Mirzapur region of Uttar Pradesh – and represent probably the widest range of both aesthetic and structural quality in contemporary Indian rugs. At their best, Indo Mirs are as good, if not better, than anything bearing this design produced in Persia today; and at their worst, they are among the shoddiest items on the market. It is therefore crucial to establish the merits of each individual item.

Most Indian rugs using this design are marketed as Indo Mirs or Indo Serabends, depending on whether an allover (*mir*) or diamond-shaped central medallion (*serabend*) has been employed, although it is not unknown for them to be named after other Persian groups who use the *boteh* in their designs. Some Indo Mirs are produced in the traditionally Persian reds and burnt orange – although often in slightly more pastel shades – but many use either autumnal ochres or softer shades of champagne and ultramarine. Indo Mirs are made in a wide variety of sizes, including runners and large carpets. Today the vast majority of Mir and Serabend rugs coming onto the market will have been made in India, rather than Persia.

Resale value Good quality Indo Mirs are excellent value for money, but are unlikely to prove profitable investments.

ISFAHAN (pl. 36)

Country: Persia (Iran)

Category: workshop and masterworkshop

Price range: high to wealth

General details The ancient city of Isfahan in central Persia produces what are arguably the most consistently fine wool-pile rugs made anywhere in the world today. Their quality may be matched by individual items from the other major Persian workshop groups, but Isfahan produces far fewer poor quality rugs.

Isfahans are knotted on either silk or cotton foundations, with up to 400 Persian knots per in², using exceptionally good quality (often Kurk) wool for the pile, which is normally clipped quite low. The appearance of Isfahans produced in the last 50 years, under the Pahlavi influence (p. 95 and pl. 36), is radically different from those made in the later 19th and early 20th centuries. These older items tend to employ a richer palette and more varied designs, and because they were made under the Qajar dynasty, they are sometimes referred to as Qajar-style Isfahan rugs.

In contemporary items the palette is normally more pastel, and technical perfection is generally of greater importance than artistic flair. Contemporary Isfahans are, however, extremely attractive, and the subduing of the palette, particularly the elimination of strong reds, makes them more compatible with Western decorative schemes.

A range of traditional designs are still used – including allover Shah Abbas, vase, tree-of-life and pictorial schemes – but by far the most popular composition is based on a circular central medallion (derived from the famous mosque of Shah Lutf Allah in Isfahan) set against an elegantly sculpted field decorated with intricately purling vine, palmette and floral motifs (pl. 36). The most popular colours are blue, white, pale mushroom and beige, but almost every other colour and tone may be used, particularly in masterworkshop items.

The most famous name in Isfahan weaving is undoubtedly Serafian, although both Hekmatnejad and Haghighi have produced a number of items worthy of the master himself; Emame, Shahapour and Asatchi are also masterweavers of note.

Masterworkshop items are made in a wide range of sizes, including extremely large carpets, and are far more varied and innovative in their designs. Standard workshop rugs are generally made in smaller sizes – c. 6' × 4' (1.83 × 1.22 m) being the most common – but room-size carpets are also made. Both workshop and masterworkshop items are frequently inlaid with silk – either as outlines on individual motifs or as large segments of the field – but rugs made entirely in silk are rarely found.

Resale value A good quality Isfahan is generally considered an assured investment, but the market in workshop items can be particularly volatile, and the less exemplary items cannot be guaranteed to increase in value.

JAIPUR (similar to pl. 33)

Country: India

Category: workshop

Price range: low

General details Made in and around the city of Jaipur in Rajasthan, they epitomize the medium grade items made in India. They are woven on cotton foundations, with up to 160 Persian knots per in^2, using reasonable quality wool normally clipped medium to medium/high. Jaipur compositions are almost equally divided between traditional Caucasian and Persian – particularly medallion-and-corner and vase – designs, but Caucasian schemes tend to be more successful because Jaipur knotting is not quite fine enough to do justice to the more intricate and curvilinear Persian designs. They are similar to Mori Kashans and Kashmir rugs, but are less sophisticated in the articulation of the designs. The palette is also roughly divided into schemes dominated by reds and blues, and those which employ autumnal shades of beige, brown and gold, the latter being more prevalent in Persian designs. Jaipur produces items in a wide range of sizes and shapes, including runners and large carpets. They are normally marketed as Jaipurs, but, as is common in India, may also be sold under the name of the Caucasian or Persian group most closely associated with the specific design.

Resale value Jaipurs represent good value for money and should be purchased as sound furnishing items, rather than investments.

KARS (pl. 19)

Country: Anatolia (Turkey)

Category: village

Price range: low to low/medium

General details Made in a number of villages, mainly in the Armenian part of Turkey, near the Russian border, they are almost exclusively based on old Caucasian, or Caucasian-inspired designs. They are generally well made, with a knot-count of 70 to 120 per in^2, on traditional woollen foundations and the pile wool, which is normally clipped to medium length, is of good quality. Although their designs are usually based on the bolder, more heraldic Kazak amulet/medallion schemes, the Kars palette is far mellower than that used in the Soviet Union, and you should have no difficulty in distinguishing a Kars Kazak from a Russian Kazak. This combination of bold designs and pastel colours is extremely attractive and eminently compatible with most Western decorative schemes. Kars rugs are usually marketed under the name of a design or town (e.g., Kars Kazak or Kars Nigde) but they may be simply referred to as Kars. They are made in a number of sizes, but *seccade* dimensions are most frequently encountered, and large carpets are quite rare.

Resale value Kars are good value for money, but will probably not increase in value as much as more traditional Anatolian rugs.

KASHAN (pl. 34)

Country: Persia (Iran)

Category: workshop and masterworkshop

Price range: medium/high to wealth

General details The reputation of rugs made in the central Persian city of Kashan was so high that, according to Persian folklore, it was considered a compliment to say that a person came from Kashan, for this implied that they possessed quality and style. Contemporary Kashans are among the finest rugs produced today, but the standard of individual items varies rather more than it does with Isfahans, and it is important to assess each item on its own merits. They may be woven on either cotton or silk foundations, with between 200 and 400 Persian knots per in^2 (pure silk items may have 600 or more). The pile wool, which is normally clipped quite low, is silky and of very high quality. Kashan designs have changed less under Pahlavi influence than those of many other Persian workshop groups. Items are still produced in traditional colours and compositions.

Their most common design is a sculpted, diamond-shaped central medallion, set against an intricately purling palmette and floral field (pl. 34), but allover Shah Abbas, vase, hunting and pictorial schemes are also found. The traditional palette is dominated by rich reds, blues, ivory, yellow ochre, burnt orange and occasionally green, although more recently Kashans have been produced in much paler, pastel tones. These latter items are usually referred to as 'five-colour Kashans' and, with their soft bluish greys, are specifically designed for the Western market. Kashans are made in a wide range of sizes, but the five-colour Kashans are more likely to be found as room-size carpets than as smaller rugs. The most famous names in Kashan weaving are Mohtaschem and Atasch Oglou, but as Kashan rather missed out on the Pahlavi boom, there are few contemporary weavers who can justifiably be elevated to the masterworkshop class.

Resale value A good quality Kashan, whether wool or silk, is generally considered a very sound investment, but all Persian workshop carpets are susceptible to fluctuations in the market, and their resale potential is not as assured as it once was.

KASHMIR (pls. 31, 32)

Country: India

Category: workshop

Price range: low/medium to medium/high

General details Made in a number of workshops throughout the Kashmir province of northern India, Kashmirs are generally regarded as the finest items made on the Indian subcontinent today. Kashmir is equally renowned for both its wool and silk items, and the best quality examples are as good as, and sometimes better than all but the finest contemporary Persian and Anatolian workshop rugs. Knotting can be very fine, with *c.* 322 Persian knots per in² as an average on the better items, and even higher knot-counts on silk and part-silk rugs. The materials are generally of reasonably good quality. Unfortunately, a number of inferior items, employing the *langri* knot (which literally means 'lame woman', and is the Indian equivalent of the Persian *jufti*

knot), are also produced, either in Kashmir itself or the neighbouring states of Punjab and Uttar Pradesh, and it is therefore extremely important to check each rug carefully.

The weaving tradition in the region dates back to the 16th century and possibly earlier, but contemporary Kashmirs are made almost exclusively in Persian-inspired medallion-and-corner, vase, paradise, prayer-rug, hunting, panelled garden, *zel-i-sultan*, allover floral and Shah Abbas designs. In addition, a number of (frequently good quality) copies of famous carpets are produced (pl. 32).

Srinagar, the capital, is noted for its high quality silk rugs, which can normally be distinguished from other silk items by their rather stiff handle. As inferior pieces are sometimes passed off as silk Srinagars, always check the knotting and the general 'feel' (which should not be too floppy or soft). All Kashmirs are woven on either cotton or silk foundations, and the pile, whether wool or silk, is usually clipped fairly low. The palette is less pastel than that of other Indian and Pakistani weavers, but the shades are still paler and more contrasting than those in most Persian rugs. Silk Srinagars are mainly made in small rug sizes, but Kashmirs, whether silk or wool, come in a wide range of sizes, including quite large carpets.

Resale value Kashmirs are usually very good buys, but they lack the mystique of Persian rugs, and are consequently not viewed as potentially collectable. However, the better quality items have probably the best chance of any Indian rugs of holding their value over the longer term.

KAYSERIA (similar to pl. 30)

Country: Anatolia (Turkey)

Category: workshop

Price range: low/medium to high

General details Made in a number of villages around the towns of Kayseria and Sivas, in central Anatolia, and noted for the variety and inventiveness of their designs. Both silk and wool items are produced, and the quality of the materials and standard of craftsmanship are generally high. Woollen pile items are normally woven on cotton foundations, with 80 to 240 Turkish knots per in^2, and silk-pile items may have either cotton or silk foundations, with up to 450 knots per in^2. The Kayseria weavers also produce rugs with a mercerized cotton pile, usually marketed as 'art' (or artificial) silk.

Kayseria designs are based on a number of traditional Anatolian (primarily Ghiordes) and Persian (mainly Tabriz and Isfahan) compositions and contain both intricate curvilinear and simple geometric schemes. Rich reds, blues, greens, yellow and gold ochres, as well as ivory, are the dominant colours.

Kayserias are generally regarded as being second in quality to Hereke, amongst Anatolian rugs, and the finest silk items are sometimes passed off as Herekes by less scrupulous members of the trade. They are normally made in a wide range of sizes, but silk and mercerized cotton items tend to be more common in smaller dimensions.

Resale value Kayserias can vary in quality, but the finer items, particularly silk rugs, should hold their value reasonably well. Only the very finest examples should be considered as investment pieces.

KERMAN (pl. 40)

Country: Persia (Iran)

Category: workshop and masterworkshop

Price range: low/medium to wealth

General details The city of Kerman in southern Persia produces some of the most refined and elegant rugs made today. They are usually woven on cotton foundations, with between 196 and 400 Persian knots per in^2, and the pile wool is generally extremely good. However, their quality is not as consistent as that of some other Persian workshop groups, and some very poor calibre items are also produced. Silk is rarely used.

Kerman is generally considered to be the main source of the most beautiful and inventive Persian designs; even today, their repertoire is unrivalled. Kerman designs can be separated into two broad stylistic types: the

first group may be described as 'traditional' and includes mainly floral-inspired interpretations of medallion, vase, panelled garden, tree-of-life, pictorial (pl. 40), hunting and *boteh* designs; the second style is often referred to as 'American' because it was developed for the American market during the late 19th century. American Kermans produced today almost always have either an Aubusson or Koran medallion-and-corner arrangement set against an open field. Their colours are both lighter and more vibrant than those employed by most other Persian workshops (with reds, blues, greens, champagne and turquoise being the predominant field hues), and the woollen pile, which is normally left quite long, is frequently subjected to a glossy chemical wash. These are generally the poorest Kermans currently produced (known as 'bazaar quality' in the trade), and it is not uncommon for the monochrome areas of open field to have been woven by looping, rather than knotting the pile yarn, which detracts from the rug's durability.

The more traditionally designed Kermans, particularly those from the small town of Ravar (or Laver, as it is often called) are normally of a much higher standard; a good Ravar may be as fine as anything made in the country today. Traditional items tend to have a shorter pile and are justifiably at the top end of the Persian workshop range; some individual items may be of masterworkshop calibre, in particular those made by Arjemand. All Kermans are made in a variety of sizes, but American Kermans are more common in large carpets.

Resale value The investment potential of a top quality Kerman rug is as high as that of any other major Persian weaving group. Traditional designs should hold their value better than American schemes.

MALAYER (similar to pl. 35)

Country: Persia (Iran)

Category: village

Price range: medium/high to high

General details Contemporary rugs from the Malayer region of west central Persia should not be confused with the old Malayer Ferahans, which are no longer made. They encompass the works of a number of village weaving groups in and around the small market town of Malayer, and are generally very well made, using top quality pile wool and mainly vegetable dyes. Although they are not among the most finely knotted Persian rugs, they are soundly constructed and durable.

Malayer designs are similar to the more traditional Sarouk schemes (pl. 35) but slightly coarser and more geometric; some villages in the region produce items closer in appearance to those from Borujird or Borchalu. The most common ground colour is dark blue, but rust red and cream are also used, and a number of paler blues, reds, yellow ochres and burnt orange are introduced as secondary shades.

The town acts as a collection centre for the surrounding villages and, although some rugs are marketed under their village names, the vast majority are simply referred to as Malayers. They are rarely larger than c. 7′ × 4′ (2.13 × 1.22 m).

Resale value Good quality Malayers keep their value reasonably well.

MESHED (similar to pl. 34)

Country: Persia (Iran)

Category: workshop and occasionally masterworkshop

Price range: low/medium to medium/high, occasionally high to wealth

General details Meshed is the capital of the Khorassan province of north-east Persia and until the mid-20th century was noted for producing some of the finest carpets in the world. In recent years, the standard of Meshed weaving has declined. The vast majority of Mesheds produced today are of medium quality – with only 100 to 200 Turkish or Persian knots per in^2 in not particularly hard-wearing wool – and their designs often lack the skilful articulation of form and tonal balance that is the essence of all good Persian workshop rugs.

The repertoire is dominated by medallion-and-corner schemes in dark reds and blues, although lighter shades are sometimes used. They are similar to a classic Kashan, but the shape of the medallion may be circular or oval, with similarly contoured spandrels; the field is nearly always decorated with Shah Abbas motifs, although *herati* patterns are sometimes used, and the colours are normally darker.

Meshed produces some small rugs, but most of their output is confined to larger room-size carpets. Some Mesheds which employ *herati* decorations may be marketed under the more general heading of Khorassan. Indian weavers produce copies of Meshed schemes.

Emoghli is the most famous name in Meshed weaving. There are no contemporary weavers of his calibre, but Sheshkalani produces some very fine items.

Resale value The investment potential of an average Meshed is rather less than that of the other major Persian workshop groups, but the few fine items still produced should hold their value reasonably well.

MORI BOKHARA (pls. 27, 28)

Country: Pakistan

Category: workshop

Price range: low to low/medium

General details Arguably the most popular contemporary rugs on the market. They are made throughout Pakistan, primarily in the Lahore and Karachi regions, and range in quality from extremely coarse to extremely fine. The best quality items can have anything up to 400 Persian knots per in^2, whereas the poorer rugs may have under 100, but the local wool is rather too soft for rug-making (usually even softer than that employed in Mori Kashans) and may be weakened even further by the frequent use of chemical washes, which give the better quality rugs their characteristic sheen. Ironically, the poorer quality items are normally given much lighter chemical washes, and consequently the pile fabric is less likely to be harmed. Two other weaknesses are the dyes, which tend to be rather more fugitive than most, and the thinness, and consequent frailty, of the yarns.

Designs are based largely on Turkoman *gul* motifs, with almost infinite variations being produced; more recently they have extended to include other essentially geometric Turkoman, Persian and Caucasian (pl. 28) schemes, marketed under a range of names, including Kafkazi, Jaldar and Serapi. Some Mori Bokharas use the same colours as the originals (pl. 7), but the vast majority opt for more pastel shades (pl. 27), which, in combination with the sheeny patina of the wool, enhance both their visual impact and compatibility with Western decorative schemes.

Mori Bokharas may occasionally be marketed as Tekke or Yamut rugs, depending on the type of *gul* they employ, but their pastel colouring usually makes their origins obvious; any lingering doubt can be clarified by examining the warp and weft: Pakistani Bokharas always have cotton foundations, whereas authentic Bokharas normally use wool. Mori Bokharas are made in the widest range of sizes, including runners, mats and large carpets.

Resale value Mori Bokharas are often very finely knotted and represent exceptional value for money, but the volume of production coupled with a total lack of originality in design makes it extremely unlikely that they will ever become collectable. Although they may be highly recommended for furnishing purposes, they should never be considered as investments.

MORI KASHAN (pl. 33)

Country: Pakistan

Category: workshop

Price range: low/medium to medium/high

General details Generally accepted as the best rugs made in Pakistan; in terms of craftsmanship, they often rival the more prestigious Persian workshop rugs. The name refers to a type and quality of rug, rather than the place where it was made, and these items are produced in a number of workshops in and around the cities of Lahore and Islamabad, and to a lesser degree in workshops stretching southwards to Karachi.

Their designs are based on traditional Kashan and other Persian workshop compositions, and include a wide range of medallion-and-corner, vase, hunting, pictorial and allover floral and Shah Abbas schemes. The palette is, however, vastly different to that normally associated with Persian Kashans, and Mori Kashans can be clearly distinguished from Persian originals by their almost exclusive use of pastel shades, in which beige, fawn, champagne, pale blues and ochres predominate. Richer shades are sometimes employed, but even they often have a pastel cast.

The knotting can be very fine, with up to 400 Persian knots per in² on cotton foundations, but the local wool is rather too soft for rug-making; however, even when mixed with better quality New Zealand and Belouch wool, the pile (normally clipped longer than Persian Kashans) goes only some way towards emulating the Persian originals. However, Mori Kashans can be both very attractive and well made. They are produced in a number of sizes, but reasonably large rugs and room-size carpets are most common.

This range of Pakistani items may be marketed under the name of the producing town (Lahore, Islamabad, etc.) or the individual workshop (Akram, etc.), but they are usually referred to as Mori Kashans or, occasionally, Mori Tabriz (or Isfahan, etc.), depending on the design.

Resale value Mori Kashans represent excellent value, but their investment potential is far less than that of their Persian counterparts. While they can be highly recommended as furnishing items, they should not be looked on as purely 'investment' rugs.

NAIN (pl. 37)

Country: Persia (Iran)

Category: workshop and masterworkshop

Price range: medium/high to wealth

General details The central Persian town of Nain was renowned as a weaving centre for high quality and costly woollen cloth; when this craft fell into decline around the turn of the century, rug-weavers were imported from Isfahan, and by mid-century the town had established itself as one of the foremost carpet-weaving centres in the world.

In appearance, quality and structure, Nain rugs are very similar to Isfahans, but they tend to contain more bird and animal motifs in their infill decorations, and the majority of their designs are outlined in silk.

Nains are made in most sizes, including carpets, but medium and large-size rugs are most common. The most important and influential masterweaver is Habibian, and items from his workshop are among the finest contemporary rugs produced in Persia. Masterworkshop rugs are often made in much larger sizes than standard workshop items, but they usually employ a similar range of designs and, although wool or wool-and-silk rugs are most common, some items are made entirely in silk.

Resale value Nains are generally comparable with Isfahans, but Isfahans probably have a slight advantage in investment potential due to their more consistent level of quality and worldwide renown.

QASHGA'I (pl. 3)

Country: Persia (Iran)

Category: nomadic

Price range: low to medium

General details Made by nomadic tribesmen from the uplands of the Fars province in southern Persia, who traditionally market their wares in the town of Shiraz. Old Qashga'i rugs are considered by many eminent commentators to represent all that is good in nomadic weaving, and contemporary Qashga'i items, although rarely reaching the standards of their precursors, are among the most attractive and desirable nomadic rugs made today.

The Qashga'i are a confederation of tribes of different ethnic origins, including Arabs, Kurds and Lurs; but the majority are of Turkic stock, which is clearly reflected in the Azerbaijan (north-west Persian and southern Caucasian) influence in their designs. Their repertoire is among the most varied and visually exciting of any contemporary nomadic weaving tribe. It includes a wide spectrum of *boteh*, medallion and repeating floral schemes, but the most frequently encountered are pole medallions and the *hebatlu* design (pl. 3), which derives its name from one of the sub-tribes and features a circular central medallion, repeated on a smaller scale in the four corners. Qashga'i rugs are also noted for the frequent inclusion in the field of tiny people and animals, as well as the more customary floral and vegetal motifs. The most common colours are deep reds and blues, but a variety of ochres and siennas are also used.

The knotting on the better items can be extremely fine by nomadic standards, with 200 or more Turkish (or sometimes Persian) knots per in^2, and good quality wool is normally used. Qashga'i rugs are often confused with inferior Shiraz rugs – made in and around the town of Shiraz using Qashga'i designs – and which less scrupulous dealers sometimes call Qashga'i because they can command twice the price of a Shiraz. Both groups make rugs in a variety of sizes, but large carpets are rare. The Qashga'i also produce delightful textile artefacts, including bags, camel- and donkey-trappings and *kelims*.

Resale value The finest old Qashga'i are extremely valuable and the better contemporary items are almost certain to retain their value to a high degree. A good quality Shiraz, although lacking the investment potential of a Qashga'i, may also retain its value reasonably well, but this is less assured.

QUOOM (similar to pls. 30, 31, 37)

Country: Persia (Iran)

Category: workshop and masterworkshop

Price range: low/medium to high, and sometimes wealth

General details The holy city of Quoom in central Persia is noted for silk rugs, which at their best are considered the epitome of contemporary Persian silk weaving, although relatively coarse items are also made; woollen pile rugs are produced in equally varying qualities.

Being relatively new to rug-making, Quoom has no design tradition of its own and employs the designs of other Persian workshop groups and some Caucasian, particularly Shirvan groups. The most popular schemes are medallion, Shah Abbas, vase, *boteh*, *zel-i-sultan* and panelled garden, but almost any other composition may be found. The palette is equally diverse – various shades of red, blue, green, mushroom, rose, gold and both yellow and orange ochres are employed – but the extensive use of ivory and champagne, particularly as ground colours, is a distinguishing feature. These colours may be either rich or pastel, and it is not uncommon for an antique wash (p. 27) to be used to subdue the tones and give the impression of mellowness through age. Quooms can be very well made, with between 250 and 300 Persian knots per in^2 on woollen items, and 600 or more on silk; good quality materials are normally used. The foundation may be either cotton or silk, and both materials may be used, either independently or in conjunction, for the pile.

Woollen rugs are made in a wide range of sizes, including large carpets, but pure silk rugs are usually confined to smaller dimensions. Arguably the most important contemporary masterweaver is Rashtizade, and items from his workshop are generally considered to be of exceptionally high quality. *Resale value* The finest silk Quooms may prove to have a sound investment potential, as may the finest woollen rugs, but average items probably lack the character and aesthetic authenticity needed to ensure their long-term value.

SAROUK (pl. 35)

Country: Persia (Iran)

Category: village and workshop

Price range: medium to high

General details Made in a wide area in and around the village of Sarouk in the Arak province of central Persia, they are generally of excellent quality. They are normally woven on cotton foundations, with between 160 and 400 Persian knots per in^2, using very good quality pile wool, which may be clipped either short or medium/long, depending on the design.

Sarouk designs can be separated into traditional and American schemes. The former include *boteh* and *herati* compositions – either in allover or medallion-and-corner formats – and are sometimes referred to as Serabends or Mirs (if *botehs* are employed) and Ghiassabads or Mesherikis (when the *herati* pattern is used). Perhaps the most impressive traditional design is a medallion-and-corner scheme which combines angularity with stylized, although strangely naturalistic, floral forms (pl. 35). In contrast, the American (or Lilihan) design features large blossoming floral sprays radiating outwards from a central, medallion-like floral form. It is so named because it was adapted for the American market from a design originating in the village of Lilihan; the true Lilihan design has a spidery central medallion which American Sarouks do not.

In traditional schemes, the palette is dominated by reds, blues, burnt orange, ochres and champagne, which often have a rather penumbral cast. American Sarouks use either rich rosy reds with blues and paler rose outlining the motifs, or, less frequently, bright pastel shades (usually pale blues, turquoise or lemon yellow), used to create the same strong contrasts between motifs and field as in American Kermans (p. 120).

Sarouks are made in a range of sizes, although American designs are more common in large carpets. They are generally of very good quality, but it is important to check each item because rugs from inferior groups, particularly Mahal, are sometimes passed off as Sarouks. Indian weavers produce both traditional and American schemes.

Resale value Sarouks generally have a very sound resale value, but over recent years this has proved to be more true of traditionally designed items than those which employ American schemes.

SENNEH (pl. 23)

Country: Persia (Iran)

Category: village and workshop

Price range: medium to high

General details Made in the town of Sanandaj (formerly Senneh or Sehna), the capital of Kurdistan in western Persia, which gives its name to the Persian knot – although ironically the Turkish knot is nearly always used. Senneh rugs can be very finely woven on cotton (or sometimes silk) foundations, with up to 500 knots per in^2, and the pile wool, normally clipped quite short, is of very good quality. *Kelims* are also made in the same range of designs.

The most popular composition involves the *herati* motif in an allover or, more usually, a rather angular medallion-and-corner scheme (pl. 23), but repeating *boteh* and *gul-i-Mirza Ali* (a French-inspired floral scheme which literally means 'flower of Mirza Ali') designs are also often employed. The palette is rich and penumbral, with deep reds, blues and ochres offset by paler shades of the same hues in addition to orange, white, beige and green. Unfortunately, very few Sennehs are now made and only a limited number of small rugs, and even fewer room-size carpets, come onto the market. Indian weavers produce copies of traditional Senneh schemes, particularly those based on the *herati* and medallion-and-corner formats, but these are often rather crude in both colour and design.

Resale value The growing scarcity of Senneh rugs, coupled with the quality of their weave and artistry, makes them very sound investments. This is particularly true of the finer examples.

TABRIZ (pls. 38, 39)

Country: Persia (Iran)

Category: workshop and masterworkshop

Price range: low/medium to wealth

General details Made in and around the town of Tabriz in the Azerbaijan district of north-west Persia, they represent the most variable Persian workshop items produced today. At their best they are as fine and aesthetically satisfying as the most accomplished Isfahan or Kashan; at their worst they can be as coarsely knotted and clumsily composed as an undistinguished village rug.

Tabriz rugs are usually woven on cotton foundations (although silk is sometimes used for the finest weaves), with between 80 and 400 Turkish knots per in^2. The local *Maku* wool is very strong, if a little coarse, making the better quality items sturdy and hard-wearing. The pile may be trimmed either short or medium/long, but as a general rule the shorter the pile, the better and more finely knotted the rug.

The design repertoire is arguably the most diverse and innovative in the whole of Persia, and includes interpretations of almost every Persian and universal design; but medallion, pictorial, garden (pl. 39), hunting, allover floral (pl. 38), Shah Abbas, *boteh* and *herati* schemes are the most common. In addition, Tabriz weavers have consistently evolved designs to which they have given their names (Taba Tabai, Nezam and Hady Ali, etc.). The palette is equally varied, and, depending on the market for which the rugs are destined, can be either extremely rich and vivid or more restrained in tone.

Among contemporary Tabriz master-weavers, Pour Nami is considered the finest and most influential; the masterworkshops of Sultani, Imadzadi, Nezam, Tayeh Nedjad, Shasavar Pour, Gharabaghi, Djafari, Baharestan and Mohammedi also produce items of exceptional note. Tabriz master-workshop items are sometimes made entirely in silk, but more often employ woollen piles, which may be accentuated with silk or a combination of metallic thread and silk. Both workshop and masterworkshop items are made in the widest possible range of sizes.

Resale value The finest quality Tabriz rugs are extremely sound investments, but the resale potential of the lower grades is less assured. You are unlikely to lose money on any Tabriz rug unless you were overcharged on your initial purchase.

YAGCIBEDIR (pl. 17)

Country: Anatolia (Turkey)

Category: village

Price range: low

General details These extremely attractive rugs are made in the Sindirgi area of north-west Anatolia, where they are woven in the traditional manner on a woollen foundation in good quality, close-cropped wool. Yagcibedir designs are invariably based on an elongated hexagonal 'skeletal' medallion, with stepped edges at either end, decorated with combinations of stars, large stylized birds or geometrically abstracted leaf and plant forms. The colours are usually madder red and deep rose set against a dark blue field, but occasionally blue or brown motifs may be found in conjunction with a white field. Some items, particularly runners, are composed in an allover arrangement of stylized vegetal forms, and in recent years a number of attractive items have been produced in traditional Caucasian colours and designs. The size most frequently encountered is the *seccade*, but a number of narrow runners and *ceyreks* are also made.

Resale value One of the better buys among contemporary village rugs. They are inexpensive, well made in good quality wool, and possess a distinct rustic charm that often increases with age. They are not traditionally noted for their investment potential, but the better examples may become more collectable in the future.

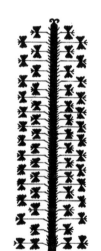

CHAPTER VII

Minor weaving groups

ABADEH Extremely attractive, hard-wearing rugs made in the village of Abadeh in southern Persia, near the town of Shiraz. They are not among the most finely knotted Persian rugs, but the knotting is very regular and, combined with the normally good quality wool, results in items of considerable durability and aesthetic merit. They are noted for their use of the *zel-i-sultan* design; most other compositions are borrowed from the Qashga'i nomads (p. 123), who have traditionally pitched their tents near Abadeh during the summer months. Colour schemes nearly always employ deep reds and blues with hints of ochre – a perfect tonal accompaniment to the simplicity of their designs. Considered good buys, because of their intrinsic qualities and the fact that they retain their value to a reasonably high degree.

AGRA City in northern India producing reasonably good quality rugs in a range of mainly Persian designs, very similar to those made in the nearby town of Jaipur (p. 118). The standard of Agra items is rather more varied, depending on whether local or Australian wool has been used. They are also produced in French- and Chinese-inspired schemes.

AMRITSAR Major weaving centre in the Punjab, generally accepted as second only to Kashmir (p. 119) in terms of quality.

ARAK Made in and around the city of Arak (formerly Sultanabad) in west central Persia, Araks are much more coarsely knotted than the rugs of their illustrious neighbours, Sarouk (p. 124). Their designs are quite similar, although rather more crudely executed, with a preference for bold floral medallions set against open fields. Although not particularly durable, they can represent quite good value for money. The average and poorer quality items are often referred to as Mahals.

ASSADABAD Village in the Hamadan district of Persia which produces fairly coarsely woven, but quite sturdy rugs in broadly geometric designs. Unlike most Hamadan village groups (p. 114), the Assadabad weavers show a preference for repeating schemes, including a bold and widely spaced interpretation of the allover *herati* design.

BASMAKCI Town in western Anatolia, whose rugs are among the best and most attractive village quality items produced in the country today. Basmakci specializes in a wide range of traditional designs from other Anatolian weaving groups – Bergama, Ushak, Ghiordes, etc. – in addition to some Caucasian-inspired schemes. They are quite finely knotted on woollen warps, using good quality pile wool, and their decorative schemes are normally well balanced and cleanly articulated. Colours tend to be more vivid than those of most other western Anatolian groups, but are generally very harmonious and attractive. Made in a wide range of sizes and moderately priced, they are usually in a slightly higher price bracket than Dobag (p. 114).

BERGAMA Town on the west coast of Anatolia which produces attractive rugs in both the sun-washed and traditional (richer) colour schemes. Designs may be either Caucasian, and resemble Kars (p. 118), or more classically Anatolian, as in Milas (p. 131) and Dosemealti (p. 114), and are comparable in quality to these groups. Some Bergama rugs are marketed as Kozaks.

BIRJAND Town in the Khorassan province of Persia which specializes in fine quality *herati*-design rugs, usually with a skeletal medallion, in a palette dominated by creams and ochres (similar to pl. 23, but with different-shaped medallion). It also produces some other traditional Persian designs. Generally considered the best rugs made in

Khorassan, although quality varies; those made in the town itself are usually better than those from the surrounding villages.

BOWANAT Village in the Khorassan province of Persia, which acts as a marketing centre for rugs woven by Arab tribesmen in the region. Similar in appearance to Qashga'i rugs (p. 123) but of inferior quality, they are normally marketed as Bowanats.

CANNAKKALE Anatolian village rugs similar to Kars (p. 118), although slightly less bold and heraldic in design.

CHELABERD High quality rugs from the Caucasian village of Chelabi, in the Karabagh region of Russian Azerbaijan, which are no longer made. The Chelaberd design – more commonly referred to as the 'Eagle' Kazak (*see* fig. on p. 105) – is still used in contemporary Russian and Anatolian rugs. (*See* CAUCASIAN RUGS, p. 105).

CHICHI Small village in the Kuba region of the Caucasus noted for its extremely attractive rugs (no longer made), which were decorated with small polygons in an allover format and possessed a distinctive border arrangement consisting of alternating rosettes and slanting bands. The famous Chichi border may be found on some Persian, Anatolian and contemporary Caucasian items. (*See* CAUCASIAN RUGS, p. 105).

CHODOR Woven by the Turkoman tribe of that name whose individual identity has largely been submerged by the other Turkoman groups in Afghanistan (p. 99). Their rugs are of excellent quality, and usually feature either a *hatchli* (*hadklu*) or traditional *gul* design.

DERBEND Capital of the Daghestan region of the Caucasus, which used to produce attractive and well made rugs (although of a lower standard than most other Caucasian groups). Contemporary Derbends represent a quality, rather than a specific group, of Caucasian workshop rugs.

DORUKHSH Small village in the Khorassan province of Persia which produces similar – but inferior – rugs to those made in the neighbouring village of Birjand (p. 127).

ERIVAN Made in the Erivan district of the Caucasus by mainly Armenian weavers. They are no longer produced but Erivan designs are still used in contemporary Caucasian rugs. (*See* CAUCASIAN RUGS, p. 105).

ERSARI The main rug-making tribe in Afghanistan (p. 109).

EZINEH Anatolian village which produces simple geometric-design rugs, very similar to Yagcibedirs (p. 125) but of poorer quality.

FERAHAN (pl. 22) District in the Arak region of west central Persia whose rugs were arguably the finest and most renowned items made during the 19th century. The name was synonymous with the *herati* composition, due to its weavers' absolute mastery of this scheme, and some dealers still refer to the *herati* as the Ferahan design. The best Ferahans were made in the village of Mushkabad, which was sacked by Fath Ali Shah shortly before the turn of the century. A handful of these old-style Ferahans are now made in the villages of Ibrahimabad and Farmahin, although they are of poorer quality than the originals. A few older Ferahans (or Ferahan Malayers, as they are often called) are still in circulation, but they are extremely expensive and rare. (*See* MALAYER, p. 120).

GEBBEH Made by nomadic and semi-nomadic tribesmen in the Fars province of southern Persia, they are among the most primitive of all Persian tribal rugs. However, the wool is of good quality and the best items possess an undoubted rustic charm. Their compositions, which show a distinct Luri influence, are usually simplified versions of the Qashga'i pole-medallion design. They may be dyed in the traditional nomadic palette of blues and reds, or use different shades of natural wool. More finely woven Gebbeh-style rugs (known as Shulis) are produced in a number of villages in the region, but often lack the character of the nomadic originals; while being decoratively pleasing, they have little or no collectable appeal. The easiest way to distinguish nomadic from village items is to examine the foundation: nomadic Gebbehs use wool and goat's hair, whereas Shulis use cotton. Both types are among the cheapest Persian rugs.

GHIORDES Town in western Anatolia which gives its name to the Turkish knot and is one of the oldest and most well known of the country's weaving centres, traditionally noted for its exquisite prayer rugs. In recent years the design repertoire has broadened to embrace other Anatolian and Persian designs. Generally considered to be better than average examples of Anatolian weaving.

GOGARJIN Kurdish village near Bidjar in western Persia which produces poorer, but nevertheless quite good quality, Bidjar-type rugs (p. 112).

HAFTMERIBAD Attractive Belouch rugs usually produced in a distinctive design, consisting of inwardly decorated vertical linear borders with some echoing horizontal motifs, similar to the *hatchli* design (pl. 10). Penumbral oranges and browns predominate, while blues and other colours are sometimes found. The quality varies, but the better items are very good value for money.

HASHTRUD Mountainous region in the Kurdish part of western Persia which produces fairly coarse but attractive *herati*-design rugs, sometimes marketed under the name of Shah Savan or Amroullah. Output is quite small; rugs are also produced in designs with a distinct Caucasian flavour.

HUSSEINABAD Village in the Hamadan (p. 114) region of west central Persia which produces medium to very good quality village rugs, usually in *herati* designs (similar to pl. 22). It is the largest rug-producer in the area, and better quality *herati*-design items from the region are often marketed as Husseinabads.

HYDERABAD Town north-east of Karachi in Pakistan, which produces medium-grade Mori Bokhara (p. 121), Anatolian- and Chinese-style rugs; its output is rarely marketed under the name of the town.

ISLAMABAD Large town in northern Pakistan which makes medium to good quality rugs, sometimes sold as Islamabads, but more often as Mori Kashans (p. 122).

ISPARTA Below average Anatolian rugs produced in pastel-toned Anatolian, Persian and even Chinese designs. Older Isparta (or Sparta) items were considered some of the finest from south-west Anatolia; contemporary rugs, although of poorer quality, are nevertheless attractive furnishing pieces.

IZMIR Important seaport in western Anatolia which acted as a major distribution centre for the carpet trade. Very few rugs were actually made in Izmir (formerly Smyrna), but its name was, and still is applied to items from neighbouring weaving groups.

JOKAR Small village in the Hamadan (p. 114) region of west central Persia which produces very fine rugs, mainly in the *herati* design, comparable to the best grade Husseinabads (p. 129).

JOSHAGAN Village in central Persia noted for its finely woven rugs and distinctive design, which features an allover pattern of flowering diamonds surrounding a central diamond. They are also produced in *minakhani* and *harshang* schemes. Finely knotted on cotton warps, in a low- to medium-cropped good quality wool pile, they are usually rather expensive. Due to their generally high standards of workmanship and the fact that production is small, they are considered very sound investments. However, quality varies and the fineness of the knotting should be carefully considered before deciding on a price. The better quality items are sometimes referred to as Meimeh or Murcecar (a nearby village). The Joshagan design is occasionally copied by other weaving groups, particularly in India and the Balkans.

JOZAN Village in the Malayer (p. 120) region of west central Persia, which produces a number of rugs in rich primary colours with a central medallion on a *herati* or Shah Abbas field. They often bear a close resemblance to Sarouks (p. 124) – and are sometimes marketed as Jozan Sarouks – but can be distinguished by their use of plain-coloured wefts; Sarouks are almost always blue. Very good quality and expensive, but with a sound resale value.

KARABAGH Southernmost region of the Caucasus, renowned for extremely decorative rugs which often featured French-inspired allover floral schemes. They are no longer made, and modern Caucasian items rarely employ Karabagh designs, but a few older examples are still on the market. They are quite expensive, but less so than many other Caucasian rugs. (*See* CAUCASIAN RUGS, p. 105).

KARAJA Made in and around the village of that name in the Azerbaijan province of north-west Persia. The proximity of the Caucasus has had a profound effect on Persian weaving groups in the region, and a strong Caucasian influence can be clearly discerned in Karaja designs. They fall somewhere between Ardebil (p. 110) and Heriz (p. 116), with a tendency to use repeating amulet/medallions similar to those of the Ardebil weavers (pl. 14), but with much more intricate, Heriz-style field decorations. They are quite coarsely woven and correspond to a medium-grade Ardebil in quality.

KARAPINAR Village near Konia in southern Anatolia noted for what is probably the most overtly heraldic of all Anatolian designs: a huge central amulet/medallion form dominating the entire field. They are very similar in character, appearance and price to Kars (p. 118). Karapinar also makes some Konia rugs (p. 130).

KASHMAR Small town in the Khorassan province of east Persia, between Meshed and Birjand, noted for fine quality rugs in the unusual *zirhaki* or 'under-the-earth' design. Kashmar is also unusual in that it tends to make more carpet-sized items than smaller rugs. In addition to the *zirhaki* scheme, medallion-and-corner rugs are produced in the Kashan style (pl. 34). Fairly expensive, but generally well made and very attractive (particularly after the brighter colours have had time to mellow). *Zirhaki* designs in particular are good investments.

KAVAK Below average quality Anatolian village rugs which specialize in tree-of-life prayer-rug designs.

KAZAK Region of the Caucasus, renowned for its magnificent, overtly heraldic rugs. Today old Kazaks are extremely rare and expensive, but a number of modern Caucasian, and Anatolian rugs are made in traditional Kazak designs. Also the name of a quality of modern Caucasian rug. (*See* CAUCASIAN RUGS, p. 105).

KHAMARIAH Village near Mirzapur in India which produces low to medium grade rugs in Persian, Caucasian, French and Chinese designs.

KHAMSEH Name of two totally unconnected weaving groups. The first is a confederation of nomadic tribes in the Fars province of southern Persia, who produce very attractive tribal rugs similar in appearance and character to those of the Qashga'i (p. 123). The second group belong to the Hamadan collective group (p. 114) and produce items similar to those of the Hashtrud.

KHORASSAN Vast province in eastern Persia which encompasses several weaving groups, including Birjand (p. 127) and Meshed (p. 121). The term is usually applied to old items from the region where exact attribution is unclear, but is sometimes applied to contemporary rugs. Weaving is often of a high standard, but poorer items are also made. The region is generally considered to be the home of the *herati* motif, and *herati*-design Indian rugs are sometimes marketed as Indo Khorassans.

KOLYAI (pl. 12) Made by Kurdish tribesmen in the Bidjar region of Kurdistan in west Persia, they spring from a similar design heritage as the universally renowned Bidjar rugs. However, Kolyai weaving is much more primitive, and their rugs are rather rough-hewn in appearance and less durable. They are nevertheless attractive, hardwearing and collectable, and considerably cheaper than Bidjars (p. 112).

KONIA Made in the southern Anatolian town of Konia, using designs based on those evolved in the nearby town of Ladik, they are sometimes referred to as Konia/Ladik rugs. Persian, mainly Tabriz, and Caucasian designs are also produced in generally more pastel shades. The wool is a little softer than that used in many other parts of Anatolia and they are not particularly finely knotted. They are, however, attractive and usually well made, and belong to the medium price range of Anatolian rugs. (*See* KARAPINAR, p. 130).

KULA Decorative rugs of fair to medium quality, made in and around the city of Kula in western Anatolia. The wool is rather soft – comparable to that used in Pakistan. Some traditional Kula and Ghiordes prayer-rug designs are still woven in the area, but most rugs employ stylized floral schemes, usually with a central medallion, in pastel shades. Kulas are in the low price range.

KURD Made by Kurdish tribesmen, and usually marketed under the name of the specific tribe (Kolyai, etc.) or village (Bidjar, etc.); items that cannot be definitely attributed are sometimes sold as Kurd or Kurdish rugs. The Kurds occupy vast and diverse areas, from eastern Anatolia through Persia and into the Caucasus, but the main concentration of rug-producing tribes is in western

Persia. Designs, colour schemes and weaving standards vary considerably, with each tribe or sub-tribe producing its own distinctive work, but they are generally of a high standard, both structurally and aesthetically, and Kurdish wool is very good.

LAHORE City generally regarded as the pre-eminent rug-producing centre of Pakistan. Its items are sometimes sold as Lahores, but more often as Mori Kashans (p. 122).

LAMBERAN (pl. 14) Small region near Heriz in north-west Persia, which produces brightly coloured, geometric design rugs similar to those produced in Ardebil, Meshkin and Karaja, with a distinct Caucasian flavour. They are rather coarsely woven, but can be quite attractive, and are usually comparable with lower quality Heriz (p. 116) and Ardebil (p. 110) rugs.

LURI Tribesmen found throughout Persia – mainly in the west of the country and the Fars province in the south – who produce superb nomadic pile rugs. In quality, their work is comparable with that of the Kurds, but Luri designs are usually based on a distinctive 'hooked' medallion, similar to pls. 1 and 14. Most Luri rugs are marketed under the name of the specific village or tribe (Bakhtiari, p. 110, etc.), but items that cannot be specifically attributed are sometimes referred to simply as Luri rugs.

MAHAL Coarsely woven rugs from the Arak region of west central Persia, but more closely akin, in both quality and appearance, to those produced around Hamadan. They are usually made in carpet sizes and belong to the medium range of Hamadan goods (p. 114). However, Ziegler Mahals belong to a different category altogether: they were made under the auspices of the Ziegler Company during the late 19th and early 20th centuries, using European-inspired designs, and are now extremely collectable and expensive.

MAMLUK Made in Egypt during the Ottoman Empire with designs based on a central octagon.

MARASALI Extremely attractive Caucasian rugs (p. 105) no longer produced. Older items are sometimes found, but are expensive.

MEHRIBAN Name of two independent Persian weaving groups belonging to the Heriz (p. 116) and Hamadan (p. 114) collective groupings.

MESHKIN Coarsely woven rugs from the Heriz region of north-west Persia, noted for their bold, Caucasian-inspired designs and earthy colouring. They can be quite attractive and cheap but are not particularly hardwearing. In appearance they are more similar to Ardebils (p. 110) than Heriz (p. 116).

MILAS Village rugs made in and around the town of Milas in south-west Anatolia, they are some of the most attractive and authentically Anatolian items produced in the region. They are reasonably finely knotted on woollen or cotton foundations using coarse but durable pile wool clipped medium to low. The most popular and distinctive design features a stylized tree-of-life motif or flowering diamond within a prayer-rug format. The borders are broad and contain elegant, highly stylized floral, vegetal and geometric motifs. The palette is usually pastel with harmonious interplays of pale umber, sienna, grey, rust, ochre and a unique shade of greenish-yellow. Indian weavers now make copies of Milas designs. Milas rugs represent very good value for money, but do not have a particularly secure resale value.

MIR The village of Mal-e-Mir in west central Persia gave its name to the *mir-i-boteh* or *mir* design (pl. 26). It no longer produces rugs, but those it did produce are now highly prized collectors' items. Similar rugs are still made in the surrounding Serabend district. Their *boteh* is normally larger and less delicate and is often employed in conjunction with a diamond-shaped central medallion. Serabends are neither as finely knotted nor as aesthetically accomplished as Mirs, but they are nevertheless attractive and durable. The Serabend palette is mainly confined to reds, blues, burnt orange, ivory, pale greens and ochres. Serabends are in the medium price range and their durability and village character could make them sound long-term investments. Indian weavers make copies of both Mir and Serabend designs. (*See* INDO MIR, p. 116).

MIRZAPUR Town in north-east India which produces low to medium grade rugs, generally inferior to Jaipur (p. 118), in a wide range of mainly Persian designs.

MOUD Finely woven items from the province of Khorassan in eastern Persia. Their designs are usually based around the *herati* scheme, with or without a central medallion. They are knotted on cotton foundations, using good quality pile wool which is usually clipped quite low, and are probably the best items made in the province. Blue and white are the most common field colours. They are made in a wide range of sizes and are generally rather expensive, but due to their quality and limited output, represent both good value and investment potential.

MUSHKABAD Principal city of the Ferahan/Arak region of west central Persia, destroyed by an earthquake in the early 19th century. The name is applied to contemporary rugs made in the district, which feature a distinctive geometric interpretation of the old Sarouk 'medallion and *herati*' design (p. 124).

MUSHWANI Belouch tribesmen from western Afghanistan who produce extremely attractive and top quality nomadic rugs in distinctive variations on Belouch designs (p. 111).

NASRABAD Rugs produced by tribesmen of mixed Luri, Qashga'i and Arab origin in mainly Luri designs, particularly elongated, pendented medallions. They are coarsely knotted, but compact and hard-wearing, and usually employ harmonious shades of light red, orange, camel and yellow ochre. Nasrabads are extremely collectable, because of their visual and structural qualities and also due to the fact that they are one of the few nomadic groups that seem to have been unaffected by commercial pressures, leaving their rugs with an increasingly rare unspoilt freshness.

NEHAVEND Village in the Hamadan (p. 114) region of west central Persia which produces a small number of coarsely woven rugs in a rather primitive geometric interpretation of the American Sarouk design (p. 124), usually in reds and blues.

NISHAPUR Tribesmen who produce some of the finest and most attractive Belouch rugs (p. 111). Nishapurs are quite finely knotted in good quality wool, and often feature a plethora of tiny animals and birds interwoven between the major, usually *gul*-like forms. Their colours are brighter and more varied than other Belouch rugs and they tend to be slightly more expensive.

OWLAD Made by Luri tribesmen in southwest Persia, they usually feature geometric medallions set against deep reds and blues. Owlads are top quality tribal rugs, made more desirable by their relative scarcity.

PAOTAO Name given to old Chinese rugs (p. 103) which contain naturalistic renditions of traditional landscape and animal forms.

PEKING (pl. 29) Chinese rugs (p. 103) featuring *Shou*, medallion, floral, Buddhist and Taoist motifs on an open field, often in blue and cream. In contemporary rugs, pictorial and Aubusson designs are also found, and a wider range of colours is used. The term also denotes a quality or grade.

QASVIN Town in the Arak region of west central Persia which used to produce very fine quality rugs almost identical to those of Sarouk (p. 124). A few are still on the market, but these are expensive and very rare.

QUCHAN Kurdish village in the mountains north-west of Meshed in eastern Persia, which produces very attractive Caucasian-style rugs. They possess a rough-hewn beauty which, in addition to the quality of the wool, makes them eminently collectable.

RAWALPINDI Town in northern Pakistan which produces Mori Bokharas (p. 121).

SAMARKAND Important Central Asian city on the old silk route to China. It became the main export centre for Chinese rugs from Khotan, Kashgar and Yarkand (known collectively as Samarkands), which are extremely rare and valuable; it is now part of the Soviet Union. Contemporary Samarkands are workshop versions of these and other old East Turkestan rugs, and combine the traditional Turkoman design repertoire – particularly the *gul* motif – with a more Chinese palette of richer pastel reds, blues and creams. They are similar to Beshir (p. 112) and Bokhara (p. 113) in appearance (pls. 7, 8), but with larger motifs and more pastel shades. The result is a fusion between the design heritage of Central Asia and China, which is both aesthetically pleasing and compatible with Western furnishings. Contemporary Samarkands are well made, produced in a wide range of sizes and comparable in price with other modern Soviet rugs.

SERAPI North-west Persian group which makes boldly geometric and brightly coloured rugs, not unlike those of Heriz (p. 116). The name is most frequently encountered when applied to certain Mori Bokharas (p. 121). Older Serapis are now very expensive.

SHAH SAVAN Tribesmen of north-west Persia who weave a number of remarkably beautiful rugs. They have much in common with the Hashtrud and Khamseh, but if anything the design repertoire is more vibrant and uncompromising. Outstanding nomadic items which will only become more collectable over the years.

SHIRVAN (pl. 24) The most famous and desirable of all the old Caucasian groups (p. 105); they are no longer made, and those still on the market are extremely expensive. Contemporary Shirvans are made in workshops throughout the Soviet weaving area, but bear only a passing resemblance to the older items of that name. In contemporary rugs the term refers to a general quality, rather than a design. (*See* fig. on p. 88).

SINKIANG Noted for its Turkoman rugs before it was incorporated into China. Some traditionally designed items are still produced in the region, but most follow the more general range of modern Chinese compositions (p. 103). Traditional East Turkestan schemes are produced in the Soviet Union and marketed as Samarkands (p. 132).

SIVAS Usually made by prisoners in the gaol at Sivas in central Anatolia. They often feature intricate Tabriz-inspired designs (p. 125), are of good quality and expensive. Very few are made. (*See* KAYSERIA, p. 119).

TAFRISH Village in the Hamadan region of west central Persia which makes good quality rugs in a very distinctive design based around a huge circular central medallion (sometimes called a clock-face medallion because of its division into segments). The colour scheme is almost always dark blue and red with cream and yellow ochre as secondary tones. Tafrish rugs are moderately priced and quite collectable. Indian weavers make copies of Tafrish designs.

TAIMANI (pl. 5) Woven by nomadic tribesmen who, although not ethnically connected, are usually considered part of the Belouch group (p. 111). Taimanis are the most coarsely woven and simple of all Belouch rugs, but they possess a distinct rustic charm, and are very inexpensive.

TASHPINAR Made by village tribesmen in eastern Anatolia. They are quite finely knotted for tribal items, using very good quality wool, and possess a primitive charm. Designs are similar to those of the Yahyali (pl. 16), although the Tashpinar medallion is more elongated, and the same range of reds, blues, umbers, siennas, ochres and greens is used. Relatively inexpensive and excellent value for money.

TEHRAN Capital of Persia, where extremely good quality workshop rugs used to be made. Few are now produced and the older ones can be very expensive. They are sometimes marketed as Veramins (p. 134)

TIENTSIN Region of China that traditionally made large carpets, usually with a brownish cast, decorated with frets, swastikas and meander designs, but never flowers. Contemporary Tientsins may or may not come from this region and feature a much wider range of designs. (*See* CHINESE RUGS, p. 103).

TUISARKAN (pl. 15) Made in the Hamadan (p. 114) region of west central Persia, they usually feature an elongated hexagonal pendented medallion, with similarly contoured corners, set against a field decorated with highly stylized floral motifs. Fairly bright colours are common, with red, blue, orange and sometimes green, predominating. Boldly attractive in both colour and design, they are generally above average quality for the region.

USHAK Coarsely woven rugs made in and around the town of Usak in western Anatolia, which are specifically designed to satisfy Western tastes. Designs include allover floral patterns, medallions and variations on Milas prayer-rug schemes, but the colours are nearly always pastel in tone. Despite the coarseness of the knotting, Ushaks use good quality New Zealand wool and are generally in the same price bracket as the more finely knotted Milas rugs (p. 131). Old Ushaks are considerably finer, and more traditionally Anatolian in design, but are quite rare and expensive.

VARANASI The city of Varanasi (formerly Benares) in north-east India produces rugs towards the lower end of the Indian quality scale (p. 101).

VERAMIN Small town near Tehran (p. 133) in northern Persia, with both Luri and Kurdish settled tribesmen, which is renowned for its finely knotted and aesthetically sophisticated rugs. The most common designs are *mina-khani*, *zel-i-sultan* and *herati*, but animal and plant forms are also featured. The palette is rich and varied, with numerous shades of red, burnt orange, ochre and blue, but the predominant field colour is usually blue. Very few Veramins come onto the market, and when they do, they are expensive. Nevertheless they are good value because of their quality and sound investment potential. Indian weavers now make copies of Veramin designs.

YAHYALI (pl. 16) Tribal rugs made in the village of that name in the south-east corner of Anatolia, which feature a squat medallion, inwardly decorated with stylized floral forms, set against a hexagonal open field. Strong reds, blues, and pale raw umber with hints of yellow ochre are the dominant colours. Prime examples of Anatolian village weaving and design, they could well become more collectable in the future. In quality they are comparable to Yagcibedirs (p. 125), but owing to their relative scarcity, are often slightly more expensive. (*See* TASHPINAR, p. 133).

YALAMEH Produced by nomadic tribesmen who occupy the Fars province of southern Persia. Their most common design is a central hooked-diamond pole medallion within a hexagonal surround, set against a field decorated with floral, animal, star and human forms; contrasting but quite light shades of red, blue, orange and ochre are used. Top quality nomadic items, quite finely woven in good quality wool, they are equivalent in price to the very best Qashga'i rugs (p. 123).

YEZD Small town near Kerman in southern Persia, which now specializes in producing rugs in Kashan designs. They are not as finely woven as Kashans (p. 118), and the wool is of poorer quality, but they are attractive and rather less expensive. Colour schemes are similar to those of Kashan, but Yezd rugs often employ a cream ground. Older items were mainly based on Kerman designs, and some contemporary rugs are still produced in these schemes (p. 120).

YURUK (pl. 1) The only truly nomadic people left in Anatolia. Their rugs are similar in character to those of the Tashpinar and Yahyali (above), but employ different medallions and a more vibrant palette, with violet and yellow ochre, in addition to reds, blues and greens, as the dominant colours; umbers and siennas are also found. A few very simple pictorial rugs and items with Caucasian-influenced designs are produced. Yuruks are not particularly finely knotted, but the wool is of good quality and the structure sound. They are normally more expensive than Yagcibedirs (p. 125), and they will probably become increasingly rare.

ZENJAN Small market town in north-west Persia which produces rugs similar to those of the Bidjar (p. 112). They are usually of inferior quality, but the best are better than the worst Bidjars and sometimes less expensive. The very finest can command exceptionally high prices.

Index

For each entry where more than one page reference is given, the most important references have been shown in **bold**. Pages on which relevant line drawings appear are in *italic*, and the *italic figures* in square brackets refer to the colour plates.

All entries relating to rug designs are shown in *italic*.